Crisis Prevention and Intervention in the Classroom

What Teachers Should Know

Victoria B. Damiani

ROWMAN & LITTLEFIELD EDUCATION

A division of
ROWMAN & LITTLEFIELD PUBLISHERS, INC.
Lanham • Boulder • New York • Toronto • Plymouth, UK

Published by Rowman & Littlefield Education
A division of Rowman & Littlefield Publishers, Inc.
A wholly owned subsidiary of
The Rowman & Littlefield Publishing Group, Inc.
4501 Forbes Boulevard, Suite 200, Lanham, Maryland 20706
http://www.rowmaneducation.com

Estover Road, Plymouth PL6 7PY, United Kingdom

British Library Cataloguing in Publication Information Available

Library of Congress Cataloging-in-Publication Data

Damiani, Victoria B.
   Crisis prevention and intervention in the classroom : what teachers should
know / Victoria B. Damiani. — 2nd ed.
      p. cm.
   Includes bibliographical references and index.
   ISBN 978-1-60709-885-0 (cloth : alk. paper) — ISBN 978-1-60709-886-7
(pbk. : alk. paper) — ISBN 978-1-60709-887-4 (electronic)
   1. Classroom management. 2. Crisis management. 3. School psychology.
I. Title.
LB3013.D335 2011
371.102'4—dc22

                                                              2010052669

∞™ The paper used in this publication meets the minimum requirements of
American National Standard for Information Sciences—Permanence of
Paper for Printed Library Materials, ANSI/NISO Z39.48-1992.

Printed in the United States of America

To Brian, who handled every crisis with
just the right measure of head and heart.

Contents

Appendixes

Introduction to the Second Edition

Since this book first appeared in 2006, the field of crisis prevention and intervention in education has changed and grown. Hurricane Katrina taught us about the intense and ongoing effect of major natural disasters, not only on schools, but on entire states, even years after the event. The tragedy at Virginia Tech revealed the vulnerability of colleges and universities to crises not unlike those that have taken place in K–12 education.

During this time, we continued to mine the lessons from prior violent events in schools and used that information to enact federal and state legislation addressing bullying and suicide prevention. National crisis intervention plan requirements, intended to integrate and coordinate the work of community organizations, first responders, and schools, formalized and unified the crisis intervention process. This period also saw the publication of a crisis prevention and intervention program designed specifically for use in schools, the PREPARE program of the National Association of School Psychologists.

The Virginia Youth Violence Project reports that, compared to the 1990s, the number of national incidents of homicides on school grounds is substantially lower; however, a review of media reports on school shootings done for this edition suggests shootings that do take place may be getting less national attention. Reports of being afraid at school have declined. Reports of bullying are down only slightly, and the number of students expelled for firearm violations at school is quite high in some states. Other forms of crises for which teachers need to be prepared, such as death of a student or educator by accident or illness, natural disasters, and national or international incidents, are, of course, ongoing.

Unfortunately, crisis intervention materials designed specifically for classroom teachers are still scarce, and their role in crisis prevention and intervention continues to be one for which teachers must take the initiative to educate themselves. With updates in crisis intervention programming and legislation; integration of recent research on school shootings and other forms of school violence; and the addition of such topics as cyberbullying, relational aggression, and the needs of military families, this second edition of *Crisis Prevention and Intervention in the Classroom* further widens teachers' perspectives on school crises and hopefully puts them in a better position to prevent and cope with these events.

Victoria B. Damiani
August 2010

Introduction to the First Edition

Most of us are keenly aware that what constitutes a crisis in schools has changed over the years. Where we once saw misbehavior, we now see unlawful behavior. Where we once saw fistfights, we now see guns. Many reasons have been cited for the change, including violence in the media, family dysfunction, impersonal school environments, and inadequate services to address the mental health needs of children. Whatever the reason, the change in school climate requires a corresponding change in teacher preparation to ensure that teachers, those who are on the front line, are capable of meeting the new challenges. Unfortunately, training programs have been slow to address these new circumstances.

This book is intended to prepare teachers to recognize potential crises before they occur and assist them in developing preventative interventions. It also outlines procedures for addressing a crisis once it happens and informs teachers about various resources available in schools and communities to assist them in managing a crisis. Teachers should plan for the problems they may face, keeping in mind that schools are still among the safest places in our society. Preparation contributes to a positive atmosphere in schools. Emotional overreaction does not.

The assumption made here is that teachers are appropriate interveners in crises affecting children and that their preparation in this area is both practical and necessary. Their long-term experience with children gives them a frame of reference useful in identifying uncommon behavior patterns. Their daily contact with the same children provides them the opportunity to notice behavior change in any given child.

Teachers are often privy to family events of the children they teach, and they are part of an institution that is a known entity in the community. All of these factors increase their chance of success in preventing and coping with school crises.

One may argue that to suggest that teachers engage in crisis intervention is to put yet one more responsibility on schools that have too much already; however, crisis has found the schools, and schools must and do respond. The issue now is one of seeking the most effective response. Crisis prevention and intervention is not psychotherapy. Indeed, paraprofessionals have been carrying out successful crisis intervention for decades. Many of these interveners have far less academic background and experience in human behavior than the average classroom teacher. With adequate preparation, the classroom teacher can be one of the most important resources for crisis prevention and intervention in the schools.

This book is not intended to represent an exhaustive review of school crisis intervention techniques. Indeed, there are many well-known approaches to crisis that do not appear at all. Only interventions deemed appropriate and realistic for teachers are included. Thorough research background on even those discussed is omitted to keep this work brief and in language that will make it useful and relevant for the classroom teacher. Those seeking a more in-depth review of school crisis intervention research should refer to the reading list at the back of the book.

The author would like to thank the students of Kappa Delta Pi at Indiana University of Pennsylvania (IUP) who supported the idea for this book and "spread the word" concerning the need for this training among preservice teachers. A good deal of appreciation goes to the Educational and School Psychology Department at IUP, which continues to provide the supportive working environment so necessary for productivity. And finally, thanks to Lee Stroud of the Portsmouth Public Schools in Portsmouth, Virginia, who saw the need for crisis intervention teams long before the media shined the light.

Victoria B. Damiani
February 2005

SCHOOL CRISES:
THE THEORETICAL AND THE REAL

CHAPTER 1

The Nature of Crisis in Schools

Work hard to find that balance between mourning the past, treasuring the present, and keeping hope for the future.

—Wong, as cited by Paine, 1998, p.16

Unfortunately, most teachers don't need an academic definition of a crisis to know what it is. A crisis is when one of your students shoots another, when your colleague's husband attacks her in front of her class, when the captain of your high school football team hangs himself, or when thousands of people are killed by a plane hitting a building in your city. Educators know what a crisis is; however, a formal definition of crisis helps us see its component parts, the factors that make a crisis so devastating.

First, a crisis is an *unexpected* event. If we analyze each of the most publicized crises in schools over the last several years, we will find that, while they all ended in tragedy, each one was enough different from the last to make it basically unexpected, at least in that form. A crisis is *traumatic*. The power of this trauma has a strong emotional impact on those involved. What makes the event traumatic is its potential to end in physical or emotional harm to those experiencing it. It is often this potential and its memory that give the crisis its long-lasting impact.

The stress of the experience leads to a temporary *loss of equilibrium*, a feeling that nothing is normal or as it should be. This loss of equilibrium is often characterized by *ineffectiveness of, or inability to utilize, former coping strategies*. Finally, a crisis carries *potential for psychological growth and psychological debilitation* of the individual.

A crisis can take many forms. Personal crises may involve such developmental milestones as graduation, marriage, or retirement. Those with more potential for psychological impact might be the serious illness or death of a loved one. Crises can also be large group events like the World Trade Center catastrophe or Hurricane Katrina. In schools, crisis events have often involved smaller, targeted groups and have included loss of life. School crises by their very nature carry a particular impact unlike crises in other forms. What is it about a school-related crisis that makes it so very wrenching to a community?

Crises in schools involve children, the very individuals a society is expected to protect. When we cannot protect our children, we feel vulnerable and experience a loss of self-esteem. We associate schools with our own time of innocence and youth. Everyone can identify with the experience of attending school, so everyone is affected when a school is involved in a crisis. A violated school environment leaves us feeling that nothing is as it was. Finally, schoolteachers and principals are mainstream people. They are just like most of us. Not everyone knows a television star or politician, but everyone knows a teacher. They are us.

For all of these reasons, crises in schools carry great potential to affect the community, influence the mental health of children, and change the view of one of society's most important institutions. Events with such far-reaching implications cannot be handled only by the mental health professionals among us. Others have to help, and few are in a better position to assist with a school-based crisis than the classroom teacher.

We all have heard about teachers who put themselves in danger to protect their charges. Any person, in any setting, who performs such an act is truly a hero; however, no one would wish more than those teachers themselves that they had never had such a terrible opportunity to show their mettle. Ideally, there is another role for the teacher, one that leads to prevention, or timely intervention, before harm comes to anyone.

Many of the school crises that have occurred are still under study, and we continue to learn from them. The crises discussed here were chosen for the abundance of public information that was available, mostly due to the media attention they received, and because they were all perpetrated by students.

Not all of the information reported may be completely accurate. The reason for reviewing these stories is to illustrate some of the different aspects of crises that took place in educational settings. The purpose is not to suggest that the event could have been prevented; however, knowing what was seen in the school prior to the occurrence might be informative as we explore the teacher's role in crisis prevention and intervention.

REAL CRISES

A Shooting in Moses Lake

According to the *Seattle Times* (Tizon, 1997), on February 2, 1996, 14-year-old Barry Loukaitis walked into his ninth grade algebra class carrying three guns, one of which was a lever action rifle. He shot and killed his teacher and two classmates. Academic records show that Loukaitis was a capable student. He reportedly wrote a poem and other writings that included statements about killing and death. After the shooting, Loukaitis's mother noted that family problems had begun two years before, and postevent reports of the boy's behavior suggest progressive deterioration in mood during that time. At one point his mother told him of her plan to kill herself.

Especially important to note was Loukaitis's described change in demeanor from a friendly and pleasant child to one who was withdrawn and mistrusting. Friends reported that he was preoccupied with death and killing and had videos, books, and music related to those themes. He was often teased and bullied at school. The bullying apparently got so bad that Loukaitis often had bruises (Tizon, 1997).

Student Kills Three in Pearl, Mississippi

On October 1, 1997, 16-year-old Luke Woodham killed two students and wounded seven others at Pearl High School. Investigators reportedly believed that Woodham was part of a group, identified in *People Magazine* as being on the "social fringes," who were also involved with the plan to bring harm to the school (Hewitt, Harmes, and Stewart, 1997). Woodham was described as a "solid A and B student who was frequently the target of taunting and ridicule from other classmates" (Hewitt, Harmes, and Stewart, 1997, p. 119). He stabbed his mother, a single parent, to death and reportedly had killed his own dog some time before the incident at school (CNN, 1998). Woodham kept a journal in which he outlined his plans and feelings of alienation, due, in part, as he explained, to the glory athletes attain for doing so little and the negative feeling that exists for those strong in intellect and academics (Hewitt, Harmes, and Stewart, 1997).

Students Killed during Prayers in Paducah, Kentucky

On December 1, 1997, 14-year-old Michael Carneal shot several fellow students, three of whom died, during a group prayer session at his high school (Malthe, Riley, Hall, and Adams, 1998). "The Paducah school principal said a postattack examination of Carneal's school essays and short stories revealed that the bespectacled 14-year-old boy felt 'weak and picked on'" (DeFlitch, 1997, p. A1). A *Newsweek* article described Carneal as the "son of a successful lawyer who wasn't into drugs or cults" (Pedersen and Van Boven, 1997, p. 30). He was a B student and played in the band (Pedersen and Van Boven, 1997).

Killings in Jonesboro

On March 24, 1998, Mitchell Johnson, 13, and Andrew Golden, 11, pulled the fire alarm and shot at fellow students and teachers as they left Westside Middle School in Jonesboro, Arkansas. Fifteen were hurt or killed. Golden reportedly owned two rifles, a shotgun, and a crossbow, and the pair obtained additional arms from the home of a relative.

Classmates described Johnson as a bully who threatened other students, but also as one who was teased about his weight. He had recently been rejected by a girl. His parents were divorced. Neighbors reported that, at one time, Johnson had shot a gun near their house, but he was also described as polite and a churchgoer. Golden allegedly came from a family of "avid shooters" but was more like a "bully's victim, than a bully himself," according to acquaintances (Blank, Vest, and Parker, 1998).

Teacher Killed in Edinboro

On April 24, 1998, John Gillette, a middle school science teacher, was fatally shot by 14-year-old Andrew Wurst at a school dance in Edinboro, Pennsylvania. Two students were also wounded. A friend of the shooter testified that he had told her weeks before that he was going to kill someone some day, like the boys did in Jonesboro. She later said she thought he was joking. He also told other friends that he planned to kill himself. After the incident, peers reported having noticed earlier that Wurst had become unfriendly and that they knew he was unhappy (Becker, 1998; Hays, 1998).

Death at Columbine High

In April 1999, Dylan Klebold and Eric Harris opened fire on class-mates at Columbine High School in Littleton, Colorado, and then killed themselves. Thirteen died, including one teacher, and many more were wounded (Able, 2004; Cullen, 2009). The boys were described by a classmate as mostly keeping to themselves and being targets of ridi-cule. They reportedly belonged to a group who wore trench coats and combat boots and resented the privileges and attention given to the athletes at the school.

Harris earlier had written a vivid description of war and death for a creative writing assignment. He also allegedly had threatened to kill students in the past (Hewitt et al., 1999). Harris was on antidepressant medication at the time of his death, and both boys had prior involve-ment with law enforcement (Cullen, 2009).

Thurston High School Student Fires at Others in Cafeteria

In May 1998, 15-year-old Kip Kinkel killed two fellow students and seriously wounded 25 others one day after he had been suspended from school for trying to buy a firearm from a student. (His parents had taken away his guns as a form of punishment.) He also killed both of his parents, who were teachers themselves and were described by an acquaintance as not being "absentee parents" (Barnard, 1998; Malthe, Riley, Hall, and Adams, 1998; Paine, 2002). A *Pittsburgh Post-Gazette* article further described Kinkel as living in a "big, beautiful house," as hanging out with the "preppies at school," and playing football (Foster and Prodis, 1998). He reportedly told a friend that he wanted to place a bomb under the bleachers at the school and that he had enough firepower to "hit the cafeteria." Another friend said that Kinkel seemed angry a lot and had told him that he wanted the "firepower to kill people."

On the day of the shooting, Kinkel was carrying a 22-caliber rifle, a 22-caliber handgun, and a pistol (Egan, 1998). Kinkel had been on medication for depression and had been to counseling (Foster and Prodis, 1998). Peers said that Kinkel had a temper, that he had changed in the last few years, and that he was especially angry about insults he had received from other students.

Principal and Student Dead in Red Lion

In April 2003, a 14-year-old Red Lion, Pennsylvania, student, James Sheets, who was described as carrying "multiple guns," shot and killed his middle school principal and then himself. News articles say that Sheets did not have a history of discipline problems or conflicts with the principal (Levy, 2003) and described Sheets as an "athletic boy who played on the school football team and could often be found skateboarding or shooting hoops in his rural subdivision" (CBSNews.com, 2003).

Shootings in Red Lake

In March 2005, 16-year-old Jeff Weise killed his grandfather and his grandfather's girlfriend in their home and later a school security guard, five students, and himself at Red Lake Senior High School. He was reportedly carrying three guns at the time. The school is located on an Indian reservation in Minnesota, and both of Weise's parents were Native American. Weise had posted on a Nazi-related website prior to the killings (CNN.com, 2005). Students said he was teased at times. He was alternately described as quiet, wearing a trench coat, an introvert, and as being "just like any ordinary student" (Gunderson, 2005). His father died by suicide in 1997, and his mother had been in a nursing home for several years after an automobile accident (Gunderson, 2005).

California Shooting Called a Hate Crime

In February 2008, 14-year-old Brandon McInerney was charged with the shooting death of 15-year-old Lawrence King. The shooting took place in a junior high classroom and was said to be related to a prior confrontation between the students related to the victim's sexual orientation. The shooter was described as a good student with no criminal history. McInerney's father was described as having had "brushes with the law" (Saillant and Covarrubias, 2008). The school district said that they had offered counseling to both parties because they were aware of their problematic relationship (Saillant and Covarrubias, 2008).

WHAT WE CAN LEARN[1]

Risk Factors

Does this information tell even the wisest teacher where and how to find the next troubled child? I don't think so. If it tells us anything, it should be that the clear profile or clear prediction of trouble ahead does not exist. Let's look at some of the factors that statistics tell us could put youth at risk.

One factor is living in a single-parent family. Did the shooters come from single-parent homes? Some did, and some did not. Some came from families considered to be traditional and concerned. A comprehensive study carried out by the U.S. Secret Service and Department of Education (hereafter called the Safe School Initiative) that looked at 37 major incidents of school violence between 1974 and 2000 found that 63% of the perpetrators came from two-parent families (Vossekuil, Fein, Reddy, Borum, and Modzeleski, 2004). Another risk factor is academic difficulty. Did the shooters have academic difficulties? As far as we can tell, most of them did not. The Safe School Initiative also found few attackers to be failing in school. Poverty is another risk factor. Did the shooters come from low-income families? It would seem that most of them did not. Difficulty with peer relations in youth is considered an important risk factor for social/emotional adjustment problems even later in life. Did these students have difficulty with peer relations? From the limited evidence that we have, it would seem that most of them did.

In a 2003 study of 15 incidences of lethal student-on-student violence (some included here and some not), researchers concluded that "twelve of the cases involved an ongoing pattern of teasing, bullying, or ostracism" (Leary, Kowalski, Smith, and Phillips, 2003, p. 210). Being the victim of bullying and harassment was also an important characteristic of perpetrators that emerged from the Safe School Initiative.

Emotional problems in the family and difficult relations with parents and other authority figures are two additional risk factors suggested by the mental health literature. There is little evidence of this type available in the media coverage of these crisis events. We know that one of the shooters, Barry Loukaitis, was told of his mother's suicide plan.

Jeff Weise's father reportedly committed suicide, and his mother was in a nursing home. Brandon McInerney's father reportedly had some legal problems of his own. A few of the students, like Kip Kinkel, were in trouble with their parents and their schools; however, it could not be said that a clear pattern of family problems has emerged (Leary, Kowalski, Smith, and Phillips, 2003).

The fact that characteristics commonly considered to be risk factors would not have been much help in identifying these students does not mean that the factors are useless or that they are without foundation; however, while they may be predictive for large groups of people, this is not necessarily so for any one individual. My grandfather started smoking Lucky Strikes without filters at age 13 and did so until he turned 80; nevertheless, smoking unfiltered cigarettes is still a causative factor for illness and early death. It just wasn't for him.

There are at least two other problems in predicting violence by looking for general characteristics. One relates to the aforementioned statistical issue. Thousands of people have smoked, and that allows us to amass a great deal of information about smokers. Very few students attack others at schools with serious intention to harm or kill. Those small numbers do not give us enough information to safely generalize and predict behavior from one group to the next. This is one reason why lists of student characteristics are not very useful in predicting school violence (Burns, Dean, and Jacob-Timm, 2001).

Another problem is that there are various types of violence and different types of perpetrators. Students most likely to be involved in community gangs, for example, are not a lot like the school shooters in the previously discussed incidents.

Intuition

So, if knowing risk factors would have been little help in preventing these violent incidents, how about the "gut feeling" some folks have about being able to discern a youth who will get in trouble from one who will not? What about those trench coats, for example? Might the way a student dresses suggest the potential for trouble?

One of the boys was even known to wear a coat and tie on occasion, and there is no evidence that suggests that there was any commonality in dress or appearance in the others who participated in the violent events. One exception is that some of shooters were overweight, a factor that might have been related in that it contributed to making the students the subject of ridicule among peers.

How about the strength of character that many believe comes from sports and identification with religion? There is some evidence that participation in sports and religious activities may enhance prosocial development in youth; however, a few of the youths did belong to churches, and some did play sports. We must be careful about making generalizations. Some researchers have expressed concern that focusing on what we think are indications of trouble, based on our personal biases, can actually prevent us from noticing more meaningful signs (Reddy et al., 2001).

Signs

It would seem that trying to predict who will be violent based on risk factors and personal characteristics, often known as profiling, is not very productive. The number of false positives it could yield, that is, expecting violence from an individual or group just because they have the risk factors, could be very problematic. Imagine the potentially negative impact of identifying certain students as "at risk" for killing peers or teachers.

The approach this book espouses, instead, is an awareness of, and attention to, the signs that suggest difficulties in any one individual. The most effective signs are not demographic but rather are signals related to such negative feelings as anger, shame, desire for revenge, and fear. If we look for these signals in the aforementioned students, we may see a few important ones; however, even any one of these taken alone cannot be considered predictive with complete accuracy.

Of all of the signals provided by the shooters, the *announcements of their plans* were the most important. What we say we will do is a good, if not always foolproof, indication of what we will do. The specificity of a plan is further indication of intent. Someone who describes a plan to kill others by placing a bomb under a bleacher is likely to have given the act more thought than someone who makes a general threat. One of the youths reportedly said he would shoot in the cafeteria, for example.

Another important signal is *past behavior*. Many of these students had shot guns, so when they said they were going to shoot, they were announcing a plan for a behavior that was already in their repertoire. Another way of saying that is, if they had shot a gun before, they were more likely to do it again than someone who had never shot a gun. Past behavior was also a factor with the young man who had killed his dog, especially in the brutal way it was reportedly done. He had killed before. Harming animals is an important sign of potential for violence against humans.

Negative affect, that is anger, a desire for revenge, hate, and intense shame, all increase the potential for acting out. When the signs take place in the presence of these feelings, the potential for violence is increased. Some of the shooters are described as having acted without emotion. These impressions may indeed be accurate, especially if the youth in question had an emotional disturbance, some of which are accompanied by flat affect. Yet, emotion is expressed in the writings of some, and it is mostly negative. As would be expected, several of the students in question had strong and negative reactions to being *objects of ridicule* or believing that they were.

Awareness

One must be struck by the intensity of the feelings expressed by some of the shooters, both before and after the incidents. As a mental health professional, I am very concerned about the level of pain experienced by these students and must wonder if more attention to their needs could have revealed the intensity of their feelings, even if not the specificity of their plans.

The Safe School Initiative found that almost all of the attackers had experienced some kind of loss before the attacks. Would a chance to discuss their feelings have reduced their intensity? Might awareness of an adult that these youngsters were so bothered have led to intervention by a mental health professional who could have helped? We know a few had counseling, but several had experienced depression. There is some indication of other emotional illnesses as well, but the evidence is inconclusive.

Was the bullying of some of these students ever noticed by the school or addressed by school officials? Were adults aware of the number and degree of lethality of the weapons these children had? Are there enough well-trained teachers and mental health professionals available in our schools to detect and tend to such a high level of disturbance in our youth? This book is written in the belief that while we cannot prevent every tragedy, we can do more, and the well-trained teacher is a good place to start.

Societal Issues

There are cultural factors that arise in any discussion of the school crises our society has experienced. All of the shooters in the previously mentioned incidents, and in those occurrences studied for the Safe School Initiative, were boys. Are there gender issues here that relate to the pressures on and mental health of our boys?

What about guns? The one thing each of the students had in common was access to firearms. Availability of lethal means has consistently emerged as an important contributing factor in youth violence (Gould and Cramer, 2001). "Firearms are used in 75 to 80% of homicides and most suicides involving youth" (Osher, Dwyer, and Jackson, 2004, p. 92).

Are schools providing privilege and recognition to one segment of the student body at the expense of another? Is there some anti-intellectualism in our schools? Is there so much violence in society that it is bound to be in schools, since it is everywhere else? Is the media fostering and providing specific direction for violent acts?

Such issues are beyond the scope of this book. Most teachers have an opinion on these issues, and many do work for change; however, change is slow. In the meantime, we must work child by child and family by family as the need arises. Helping the teacher become better at doing just this is the focus of the rest of this book.

SUMMARY

In this chapter, we outlined a formal definition of crisis and the circumstances surrounding some well-publicized school crises. These events suggest that predicting violent behavior through identifying the demographic characteristics of likely perpetrators is difficult. Such an approach could also have negative consequences. A better approach is awareness and attention to signs that suggest difficulties in any one individual. The most important of these are announcement of plans, past behavior, negative affect, and being the object of ridicule.

NOTE

1. Hindsight is 20/20, and this analysis is in no way intended to suggest that parents or school personnel were negligent.

CHAPTER 2

A Crisis Role for the Classroom Teacher

One need not be a therapist to be therapeutic.

—Blom, Cheney, and Snoddy, 1986, p. 11

WHY TEACHERS?

Most of us would agree that the responsibilities borne by schools have grown over the years. Schools teach about sex, dispense medications, provide meals, transport students, and distribute applications for a multitude of public services. Could it really be appropriate to ask schools, especially teachers, to do one more thing? There is a fundamental difference between these other services and crisis intervention. That difference is that no one has decided crises should be dealt with at school. They have just happened. Schools have no choice but to cope.

A study involving 926 Florida teachers carried out in 2000 found that 47% had experienced two or more of the following incidents: "homicide of a classmate, suicide of a classmate, accidental death or injury of a classmate, news of a tragedy, or a direct/indirect threat from the community" (Jaksec, Dedrick, and Weinberg, 2000, p. 14). If we include the broad range of such possibilities as staff or student death, natural disasters, and violence at school, teachers can expect to face at least one crisis each year, and their lack of preparation to cope with crisis situations adds to their risk of burnout, stress, and depression (Pitcher and Poland, 1992). There is also evidence that students who have been traumatized may be disruptive in schools, and their own educational experiences may be affected (Berkowitz, 2003).

Teachers are significant adults in the child's life. The typical child spends more waking time during the academic year at school than at home. The school environment provides a broad opportunity to view the child's functioning with adults and many different children. The same opportunity is not available to parents or any other supportive professional, for example, a pediatrician or psychotherapist. The school situation provides strategic "teaching moments" that give the teacher a unique chance to help a child cope immediately, and on-site, with a negative circumstance. Of special importance is the teacher's ability to view a child over time and, therefore, note significant behavior changes. Behavior change is one of the most important signs of a need for intervention.

Teachers also have a number of resources for helping children, including school support personnel, relevant literature for use in the classroom, and an academic background that incorporates child development and educational psychology. Therefore, it is not a far reach to get teachers ready to help children in crisis or for them to move beyond traditional classroom management techniques to the provision of more direct intervention.

Many books and articles on crisis intervention and prevention are written for mental health professionals. There is no question that assessment of suicidal or homicidal potential, as well as diagnosis and interventions for depression and other forms of mental illness are difficult, even for that specially trained community. How can teachers, not trained in mental health issues, be expected to engage in crisis intervention and management?

Teachers should not be expected to become psychotherapists. But, in an extensive study of the effects of psychotherapy with children and adolescents, researchers found that "paraprofessionals (typically parents or teachers trained in specific intervention methods) generated larger treatment effects than either student therapists or fully trained professionals" (Weisz, Weiss, Han, Granger, and Morton, 1995). The authors go on to say that the implication here is not that professional therapists are ineffective, just that, given training and careful selection of clients, paraprofessionals can have substantial success in helping children and adolescents.

However, we don't need research to tell us that teachers can and do influence the social and emotional lives of their students. The role for teachers with regard to crisis prevention and intervention includes the following:

- utilization of research-based prevention techniques in the classroom
- awareness of students in need before a major incident occurs
- assistance in addressing the needs of the great majority of students who experience trauma but are not sufficiently incapacitated to require professional treatment or who do not have access to treatment
- provision of the ongoing, day-to-day support children need in times of crisis, whether or not they are receiving other professional services

Actually, only a small percentage of the population ever receives treatment from a mental health professional and, for many of those, the intervention comes after a serious episode requiring hospitalization or incarceration. There are still communities in the United States where mental health resources are limited. So, there is an important preventative and management role for teachers in regard to the mental health of their students.

Paraprofessional and even volunteer involvement in crisis prevention and intervention has long been a vehicle for service in community agencies (Aguilera, 1998). It is only recently that similar needs have surfaced, or been recognized, in schools. Those who know the community, are familiar to students and their families, and may share their cultural characteristics can make a significant contribution in crisis situations (Allen, Asbaker, and Scott, 2003). This is not to underestimate the contribution of professional crisis interveners, and the intent is not to replace them with teachers. But, teachers can make significant contributions to their students in a crisis, and we cannot afford to leave them untrained or their potential untapped.

Most agencies that utilize the services of community members acknowledge that certain personality characteristics are desirable in these individuals. Some of these characteristics are difficult to develop in an individual who does not possess them at all; however, most are similar to the personality factors we would hope to see in a good teacher. The personality characteristics of the effective crisis manager are as follows:

- ability to listen to others
- ability to accept emotionality in others
- ability to maintain one's own equilibrium in the face of another's emotion
- ability to take action even when experiencing stress
- ability to see another's view of an event, even if different from one's own
- willingness to improve professional skills and accept constructive criticism
- avoidance of judgmental reaction to behavior of others
- willingness to seek support for yourself

Most crisis managers, however, are made, not born, as the long history of paraprofessional training for hotline workers and Red Cross volunteers will attest. There are specific skills that teachers must master to manage or prevent a crisis, including the following:

- maintaining flexible control over crisis intervention activities
- allowing students to express themselves without being interrupted or cut off, within reason
- taking questions with an open and accepting tone
- providing accurate information at the students' developmental level
- avoiding the passing of one's own cultural or religious interpretation of events onto the students
- carrying out the practical steps one has rehearsed or learned about for use in a crisis
- respecting and protecting the privacy of others

One of the most important factors in the management of crisis situations is advance planning. A significant contribution of the school crisis prevention and intervention team is the emphasis placed on role definition, rehearsal, and anticipation of potential crisis events. Teachers must begin to think of themselves as interveners and managers in a crisis and to plan, rehearse, and anticipate so that they will be ready when the time arrives—and it will.

THE TEACHER AS SCREENER

In an excellent book intended to assist teachers in identifying stressed children and helping them cope, Blom, Cheney, and Snoddy (1986) argue that, because teachers see children in a real-life context, they have more opportunities than therapists to assess a child's social and emotional characteristics. Can teachers detect potential for problematic behavior, homicidal or suicidal action on the part of a student, for example? One must be realistic regarding the limitations even of mental health professionals to predict behavior.

A study of thinking patterns of teens carried out in 2000 suggests that homicidal thoughts are not uncommon among this age group (Crabb, as cited by Kass). Scott Poland (1989), a noted authority on suicide in schools, writes that most people have thought of suicide at some time in their lives.

So, how does one separate those who truly intend harm from those who are experiencing the usual ups and downs of life? If violence prediction were a simple matter of listing the characteristics to look for, computers could be utilized for identifying students at risk. An article by Mulvey and Cauffman (2001), entitled "The Inherent Limits of Predicting School Violence," is worth quoting here for the relevance it has to the role of the classroom teacher.

> Preventing violent incidents at school does not require . . . more sophisticated methods. . . . It seems to rest largely on developing a positive and supportive organizational climate in a school . . . a school environment where ongoing activities and problems of students are discussed . . . such an environment promotes ongoing risk management, which can be achieved only with the support and involvement of those closest to the indicators of trouble." (p. 800)

What the authors are addressing here is the importance of students feeling connected to the school and having meaningful relationships with others in the school environment. Those relationships begin with the classroom teacher. When these relationships are in place, the potential for heading off problems is enhanced. The teacher and the school screen, not with a list of identifiers, but through a connection with students. Even under those circumstances, of course, we must be aware of our limitations.

THE TEACHER AS PSYCHOLOGICAL SUPPORT

It has become clear to mental health professionals that the way an individual interprets, labels, and thinks about an event has lasting consequences on the individual's eventual adjustment following that event (Dattilio and Freeman, 2000). Children who blame themselves for a parent's divorce, for example, are likely to have more difficulty adjusting to the divorce. Students who believe they should have recognized the signs of suicidal ideation in their friend and could have saved the friend are likely to be at risk for problematic emotional reaction to the friend's death.

Teachers are in a unique position to provide accurate information to students about stressful events and help them interpret those events in ways that will lead to better mental health. A teacher can help a bullied student see that the problem may be with the bully, not the victim. In crisis events, like an earthquake or a shooting, teachers can communicate accurate information, help students study the event, or aid them in expressing their feelings in a constructive manner.

THE TEACHER AS COMMUNICATOR

Usually when we hear the term *communication* we think of expression of our own thoughts or ideas to someone else. The wise classroom teacher will consider communication from the point of view of receiver rather than transmitter. Many violent acts among youth, whether directed at self or others, are characterized by some prior sign. Often these signs will be revealed to peers rather than adults; however, visible, aware teachers may detect subtle changes in group or individual behavior. Caring teachers are also more likely to be seen as supportive individuals in whom students can confide. Helping young people trust enough in surrounding adults to reveal student plans for violence is an important prevention method.

Language arts teachers are often in a particularly advantageous position for learning about their students because of their access to students' creative writing or journals. They may detect signs of depression or hostility in student writing. After one high school psychologist did a presentation for faculty, referrals from English teachers increased considerably. While not every referral prevented a crisis, each one represented detection by the teacher that a student was feeling emotionally overwhelmed. Some signs that teachers of English might see are repetitive themes of loss or death in student writing; romanticizing of suicidal figures in literature or creative writing; and journal entries that emphasize loneliness, loss, or feelings of isolation.

The fostering of communication carries with it certain responsibilities for protecting the information shared and the communicator. Mental health professionals operate under clear legal and ethical standards regarding when, how, and if information about a client should be shared with a third party. While the same constraints and responsibilities do not necessarily apply to teachers, they should still consider these issues and be aware of federal and state laws pertaining to educators, as well as school board and building policies.

Some of the guidelines used by mental health professionals can aid teachers in developing their own standards. One important factor is *need to know*." This guideline suggests that personal information about a student should only be shared with others who have a need to know to serve the child. For example, if a child comes to school bruised, the school nurse is likely to have a need to know. Since nurses carry out physical exams, care for children when they are sick or injured, and are familiar with the health history of children, their awareness of the teacher's concerns about abuse or injury can help the child and possibly protect him from harm. However, if a mother has told a teacher about her husband's alcoholism and that teacher shares the information with the teacher who had the child in class last year, that would be a breach of this standard. Last year's teacher would not be in a position to help the child because she was aware of the father's alcoholism. Sharing in that context is more like gossip and less like professional assistance to children.

Another important guideline relates to privacy issues. This one could be termed *privacy protection* and involves locations and forms of communication about students and families. Teachers must be diligent in this regard, because most schools are crowded, open, institutional settings that were not designed with anyone's privacy in mind. The issue of privacy is present each day in the classroom, teacher's lounge, and hallways of schools. It is not easy to protect student privacy in a school setting, but sensitivity in this regard is essential to the expanded professional role of teachers put forth in this book.

In the classroom, concerns about a child's behavior or performance should be communicated personally and quietly at the student's desk or at the back of the room. Students should never be reprimanded in the hall where other students, teachers, and visitors can hear. Personal information about students should never be shared with other teachers in the teacher's lounge. Conversations with those who have a need to know should be held in private locations where others who do not have a need to know cannot hear.

Having spent most of my professional life working in schools, I know this is not easy. Space is limited, and "office space" is rarely available to teachers; however, discipline and restraint are the guidelines here. If important information is to be shared, time after school, in an empty classroom or counselor or speech pathologist's room reserved for this purpose, is required.

If teachers are to be helping professionals, they must behave and be treated professionally. Calling attention to your need for private locations to carry out your work is part of the advocacy role of teachers. This role is addressed more specifically in chapter 12. Privacy protection is not only an ethical issue; it is closely related to student mental health. Students who are repeatedly identified as "trouble" will develop reputations among educators, other students, and in the community that are difficult to live down. This can contribute to anger, frustration, bullying, and a whole host of other factors leading to crises in schools.

Just what constitutes personal or "*sensitive information*" is another question to consider when thinking about confidentiality and protection of student and family privacy. A good general rule to use is that information about any one child that is not available to everyone should be protected. This applies even to educationally related information.

For example, whether a student is in the band, plays football, or is in an advanced placement course for physics is general information any educator in the school might know or could find out; however, since student exam grades do not get posted throughout the school, that information should not be shared with those who do not have a need to know.

Personal family information is even more sensitive. Since team decision making is prevalent in schools, several people may have a need to know information that is not generally available to the entire faculty. That information should stay with the team and be considered sensitive or protected.

A final guideline to consider is "*duty to warn*." This applies to information revealed to the teacher suggesting that one student is planning or has planned to harm another student, teacher, or staff member. This is not to suggest that the teacher should take the warning into his or her own hands; however, knowing the procedure in the school for handling warning is essential. The point is that confidentiality does not take precedence over prevention of harm.

THE TEACHER AS MENTAL HEALTH EDUCATOR

The knowledge base in mental health has grown a lot in the last 20 years. The importance of stress management, self-messages, exercise, relaxation, and diet to our emotional states has been addressed, not just in professional literature, but in the public media. Many of these issues are included in health curricula in schools. Crises are real-life opportunities for children and youth to practice what they are taught about mental health and learn coping skills.

Teachers are trained educators who only need a little instruction on what to teach for society to take advantage of this learning opportunity for our youth. The Lodi Unified School District recommends that teachers help students recognize the importance of taking action in response to a crisis. "To the extent possible, teachers should help students see the situation as a challenge rather than a threat" (Brock, Sandoval, and Lewis, 2001, p. 61).

Teachers also instruct by modeling their own ability to express emotion, take care of themselves, and engage in constructive activity.

Brock, Sandoval, and Lewis also provide excellent suggestions for the integration of crisis response issues into secondary school course work. They suggest, for example, discussing the issues of accurate reporting and sensationalism in a journalism class, past crisis events in history and lessons learned, and stress reactions in a psychology class. For a list of activities for use in classes at all levels see Brock, Sandoval, and Lewis's book *Preparing for Crises in the Schools* (2001).

SUMMARY

In this chapter, we described characteristics of the effective crisis manager and important aspects of the teacher's role in crisis prevention and intervention. This role includes screening, psychological support, communication, and mental health education. Guidelines for the maintenance of confidentiality, important to open communication and a healthy school environment, were detailed.

CHAPTER 3

Children in Crisis: An Overview

It is time to teach each child to think before acting, to care about others, to use their words to problem solve.

—Dwyer, 1998, p. 10

Blom, Cheney, and Snoddy (1986) acknowledge the central role of the classroom teacher in helping children manage the stressors they face. Sources of childhood stress of which they say teachers should be aware are the following:

- human relationships
- school events
- physical stature and status
- health
- personal psychological experiences
- accidents
- change

To ease the effect of stress on students, Blom, Cheney, and Snoddy recommend that teachers develop skill in encouraging discussion, showing positive concern, approaching parents in supportive ways, knowing when and how to set up individual communication times with children, and evaluating the intensity and duration of the stress children experience. As any teacher knows, children and adolescents are much less likely than adults to verbally identify and explain the nature of a problem or feeling. Adults must provide the opportunity for alternative forms of expression and be observant of behavior that reveals the inner life of the child. Common alternative avenues of expression for children are play, drawing, and dreams.

Brooks and Siegel (1996) note that, following significant stress, young children may become more dependent, revert to earlier behaviors such as bedwetting or an unwillingness to go to bed alone, become more aggressive in play, or engage in repetitive play. Elementary school children may have difficulty concentrating on schoolwork, become irritated with peers, or have difficulty sleeping.

For adolescents, indicators may be found in withdrawal, changes in mood, and lack of motivation. A common reaction to these adolescent indicators is that most adolescents exhibit the characteristics, whether they are stressed or not. In reality, that is not the case. In most adolescents, these behaviors are not frequent, are rarely present in more than one setting, and are periodic. For example, a teenager may spend more time in her room when at home but still socialize with peers. A negative mood may evolve out of frustration of a goal or inability to attain a desired opportunity. While the mood may seem quite overreactive to an adult and may even, in fact, be an overreaction, the negativity has a reason and eventually eases.

Gauging the seriousness of indicators for problems in children of any age is challenging and important. It is more than a matter of experience, although experience helps. It is more than a matter of knowing the individual children involved, although knowing the child helps. The following guidelines should be considered when assessing the importance of any sign that a child may be in crisis:

- *Change usually has a reason.* Any significant change in behavior should be questioned. The change does not have to be from what is usually considered a positive behavior to a negative one to be important. For example, a highly active, vocal child who becomes passive, quiet, or withdrawn could be experiencing a stressor, even though the behavior change may be a welcome one from the standpoint of classroom management. Symptoms of such psychological disorders as depression, anxiety, or eating problems may also reveal themselves by changes in weight or grooming habits.
- *Ostracized children are at high risk for emotional problems and attending crises, whatever the source of the ostracism.* Ostracism

should always be addressed and never minimized by claims that the child left out will just have to learn how to be part of the group or doesn't seem to care that he or she is not welcomed by others.

- *Academic failure is always a stressor.* This is not to suggest that all children who do not find academic success will necessarily experience a crisis; however, other such indicators as mood changes, ostracism, or threats should be given even more weight than they ordinarily would if the child's life experience is further exacerbated by academic failure.
- *Past behavior is a strong indicator of behavior to come.* This guideline in gauging indicators can be problematic if it is read to mean that only students with a troubled history can experience a crisis. That is certainly not the case; however, students with a history of suicide, aggressive behavior (toward humans or animals), emotional difficulties, or depression are more likely to engage in those behaviors again or more easily slip into a crisis-producing pattern of behavior.
- *What we say is a fairly good indicator of what we are thinking about.* If a student writes or talks about death, suicide, homicide, or revenge, this must always be taken seriously. The idea that people will not engage in a behavior if they are given the opportunity to talk about it or that people who, for example, talk about suicide will never make an attempt, is simply false.
- *Resource availability is directly related to a child's ability to cope.* Resources closely related to successful coping in children are:
  ◦ availability of adults in their lives, such as parents, extended family members, and mentors
  ◦ connection to such sustaining groups in the community as neighborhood, religious communities, clubs, and teams
  ◦ intellectual and academic capability
  ◦ community supports in the areas of mental health, physical health, and recreation
  ◦ financial strength of their families and communities

While any individual reaction may vary, there are certain common emotions, thoughts, and physiological reactions to trauma. Some are immediate, and some are more likely to be present awhile after the event. Brewin (2001) notes that immediate reactions to trauma are likely to be concern for safety and heightened sensitivity to danger. Individuals may be extremely aroused, confused, and seem to be in a daze. Later they may begin to think about why the incident happened, assign blame or feel guilt, and have repeated images of the event on their minds. After a few days, or at most weeks, those who are not to develop complicated reactions should have a reduction in these thoughts and images (Brewin, 2001).

As with other aspects of crisis intervention, these descriptions are based mostly on adults and events that have taken place outside of schools. How reactions will differ because the events are experienced by children and in or during school is difficult to say. We do know that children are influenced by adult reactions and that a negative experience is likely to be more traumatic if it takes place in a location previously considered to be safe.

Those who have had prior trauma are more likely to have a complicated reaction than those who are experiencing the crisis state for the first time (Berkowitz, 2003). For teachers, that means you can expect more intense reactions to a crisis from students who have experienced the death of a parent or abuse, for example, than from the general population of students. Or, at least, you might monitor them more carefully.

WHAT STUDENTS IN CRISIS NEED

The mental health field is still not able to provide a definitive answer to the question of what a child needs in a crisis. More information is being gathered as we experience more crises in the schools; however, research on crisis intervention, in general, has been going on for many years. We do know enough to set some general guidelines for teachers helping their students through a crisis. Of course, these guidelines must be flexibly applied with the knowledge that not everyone will react in a given way, even if statistical studies show that most people do. Consider the following principles:

- *Students need to know they are safe.* No amount of intervention can result in an improved psychological state if students feel they are in danger.
- *Students need an adult model of appropriate reactions to a crisis.* We have ample evidence to suggest that the reactions of adults in their environment have a significant impact on the way children and youth will respond to a crisis.
- *Students need accurate information provided in a way that is appropriate for their developmental level.* The provision of accurate information helps us utilize our reasoning to temper emotionalism. Accurate information dispels rumors that fuel negative responses and lessens guilt related to more complicated and difficult stress reactions.
- *Students need to know that strong reactions to a crisis event are to be expected and are not signs of weakness or emotional disturbance.* When under extreme stress, we may feel that we are "going crazy" or that our reactions are too extreme. We need to be reminded that it is the situation that is extreme and has caused a reaction in us that others also experience.
- *Students need to be monitored carefully by adults in their environment to ensure that appropriate services are provided in a timely fashion.* Teachers are in a unique position to know which children are showing intense reactions and should receive immediate attention from mental health providers. Early identification of those most in need is an important part of effective crisis intervention (Berkowitz, 2003).
- *Students need dependable school and class routines that are flexible.* The order of the school day can be a comfort to students following a crisis. In some instances, school may be the only place where order has been restored and life is predictable. That does not mean that crisis events should be ignored.

WHAT THE TEACHER SHOULD DO

All explanations to students regarding stressful or crisis events should be made in developmentally appropriate terms without belaboring the event or going into specifics unnecessary to the easing of student minds. What should be done in the classroom immediately after a crisis event is discussed in detail in chapter 11. General guidelines are as follows:

- Be specific in telling students what has been done to ensure their safety.
- Demonstrate reactions appropriate to the situation.
- Provide accurate information regarding the event.
- Dispel rumors.
- Respond to student questions honestly, and admit when you do not know the answer to a question.
- Respond with acceptance to the feelings students express.
- Explain that a variety of reactions are typical.
- If the whole class has experienced a crisis event, postpone previously planned class activities that might enhance or be affected by stress, for example, tests and presentations.

ABOUT CLASSROOM DISCUSSIONS

We address classroom discussions in more detail in chapter 11. This section offers a few general guidelines. In the not-too-distant past, mental health professionals believed it was important for people who had just experienced a crisis to talk about it. More recently, we have come to the realization that one size does not fit all. We have also learned that discussions that focus on emotion related to an event have the potential, under some circumstances, to do more harm than good.

Whether one should discuss a crisis event depends on many things, not the least of which is the willingness of the individual who has experienced the event to do so. When a discussion is held in a group, such as a class, it is important that those in the group have relatively similar closeness to the event. Closeness to the event would be defined as the degree of loss or traumatization. The best friend of a student who has died is closer to the event than those who were in his class last year. A student whose father was working at the World Trade Center on 9/11 was closer to the event than students whose parents worked elsewhere.

Applying this concept to the issue of classroom discussion, we see that if three students in the class lost close relatives in Katrina, but most of the others were out of town at the time, having a general discussion with the class could be difficult for those who had the greatest loss. It could also further traumatize those who had some distance on the event. This is not to suggest that discussions of a crisis event should not be held in the classroom; however, these discussions should be planned with the school's mental health professional in keeping with the school's crisis intervention plan. In general, the teacher should do the following:

- Determine the various experiences of students in the class with regard to the event prior to a discussion.
- Consult mental health professionals in the school to get advice on how the needs of students closer to the event should be met.
- Do not press students to describe or relive an event.
- If it is determined that engaging in activities about the event, for example, drawing, reading books or articles, or having a discussion related to the event, would be appropriate, permit students to opt out if they feel the need or if their parents prefer that they not participate.
- Plan discussions with an emphasis on an intellectual understanding of the event rather than sharing of emotional reactions or unpleasant memories.

THE USE OF TELEVISION AND VIDEO

Television and video are common in classrooms in the United States. Are they a help or a hindrance to the teacher during or after a crisis? As tools in the hands of a capable, well-trained teacher, they can make a contribution. The keys to effective crisis intervention are planning and management.

Television turned on for long periods of time in a classroom providing repetitive images of a disaster as it unfolds takes the process of intervention out of the hands of the teacher. He has no control over what the students see or hear or how it is presented. This is not effective crisis management, and the repeated images could make the process of recovery harder for students, not easier.

A review of how schools handled the 9/11 disaster tells of one middle school teacher who had her students watch television all day. She later admitted that this was a result of her own need to follow events, and not because she believed it was best for her students. Several students in the class were described as showing "significant symptoms of anxiety" (Zagelbaum, Alexander, and Kruczek, 2002, p. 5).

Video after the event that addresses the causes of a disaster and contributes to an intellectual understanding of the incident can be positive. Appropriate videos should be carefully chosen. Emotionally laden images that do not contribute to understanding should be avoided. The constructive and planned use of a well-chosen video is different from television on all day in the classroom.

DRAWINGS

For elementary school children, drawings are an effective method of expression and a starting point for discussion; however, teachers must remember that as a crisis management technique, drawing is not an assignment. No child should be pressed into drawing, nor should the class be told how or exactly what to draw. Teachers should not evaluate the drawings or compare one student's work to that of another. The teacher should also allow for drawings that appear not to be or actually are not relevant to the crisis incident.

While drawings could be used as part of a classroom activity related to a crisis event, they should not be used to stir emotion or memories. Consult your school mental health professional if you plan to use drawing as part of a classroom activity related to a crisis so you will be prepared to keep control over the exercise and ready for issues that might arise, or so that the mental health professional can be present to assist.

DOCUMENTATION

Soon after the event, the teacher should document what has been done in the classroom and keep brief notes of student reactions. There are several reasons for careful documentation. First, disciplining yourself to keep notes will help you focus on individual students and their behaviors. Patterns of student behavior, especially those that stand out from the group, will be easier to recognize.

Second, mental health practitioners, administrators, and parents may ask for reasons why you have recommended special assistance for a student. Documentation will help make that case. Finally, in this age of litigation and accountability, you will be prepared to report on what you have done and student responses to your actions. Different situations will require different intervention techniques. Specific suggestions for use in various situations will be provided in the next section.

SUMMARY

In this chapter, we looked at the indicators of stress in children at different developmental stages and their common reactions to trauma. General guidelines were provided to aid teachers in helping their students through a crisis. The use of television, video, and drawings was discussed, and the importance of rumor control and documentation of events and interventions was emphasized.

CRISES AND INTERVENTIONS

CHAPTER 4

Natural Disasters

> Physical displacement and social disruption has been found to be the highest correlated factor related to outcomes after traumatic events.
>
> —Berkowitz, 2003, p. 298

The general impact of a natural disaster makes it one of the most challenging crises to be addressed by the teacher. In most instances of earthquake, flood, hurricane, and other "acts of God," entire communities are devastated. Such physical effects as ruined buildings, inaccessible roads, and lack of resources leave little that is dependable in daily lives.

Some students may exit the community temporarily or permanently, leaving others without their usual support system. Those who are seen as leaders or helpers, for example, physicians, teachers, and clergy, are just as vulnerable to upheaval and loss as everyone else and may not be able to provide services to their constituents. In their place are perhaps helpful but otherwise unknown people and agencies. If loss of life occurs, the hurt is obviously compounded. Additionally, community loss is often uneven, with some desperately harmed and others much less so.

However, following a natural disaster, community unity and mutual support are often high, and this provides a positive atmosphere for sharing among students. Natural disasters also lend themselves to opportunities for learning about causes of the disaster and helping those in need. All of these factors make the schools an appropriate arena for meeting student and even community needs in the wake of a natural disaster.

Pitcher and Poland (1992) provide some excellent ideas for use in the classroom following a natural disaster that are both academic and supportive. These interventions help the schools get back to their mission of teaching and learning without ignoring the emotional needs of their students. Some of the ideas include drawings and short stories relating to experience of the disaster, carrying out studies of the causes in science class, or studies of emotions and coping mechanisms in psychology class.

ACCURATE INFORMATION

Because feelings of a loss of control over one's life can be so powerful after a natural disaster, it is important to provide knowledge to children. Young children, especially, can misinterpret storms, earthquakes, or floods as being a consequence of their misbehavior. Older children may fear recurrence. Providing accurate information about causes can reduce anxiety and helps the child form healthier cognitions about the event.

Lessons on what to do if a similar event happens again also help to increase a sense of mastery. If the event is rare and unlikely to occur again, it is good to explain exactly how rare the event is with the use of numbers and examples. Natural disasters provide an opportunity to teach students the importance of knowledge and information in effective crisis management, from both a societal and personal point of view.

COMMUNICATION TOOLS

Natural disasters, because they are science related, allow for effective use of video as a learning tool. Video that addresses the causes of the disaster and contributes to an intellectual understanding of the incident can be positive, especially if emotionally laden images are kept to a minimum. Effective use of video as a learning tool includes student preparation, with appropriate questions to be thinking about as they view, for example, and a teacher-led follow-up discussion.

Visuals, such as photos taken of the incident or artwork related to past but similar events, can also stimulate discussion and learning, as can books or short stories. Graphs and diagrams can be useful in teaching about the frequency and magnitude of a natural event.

THE HELPING SPIRIT

Helping and contributing not only provide good civic lessons to students, but they bring a sense of closure to a crisis incident. Natural disasters provide an opportunity to develop a helping spirit in the classroom. Classes can collect money for charities, bring in materials needed by victims, and make signs and cards for first responders and those who have been hurt. When possible, these activities should be learning experiences and not just contributions. For example, does the class understand what the Red Cross actually does in a disaster? Do they know how the Red Cross got started? Combining helping and learning provides a useful and healthy model for students to use as they cope with other disasters in the future. It suggests that heart and mind go hand in hand. That model is an effective one for crisis management on both personal and community levels.

SUMMARY

In this chapter, we discussed special circumstances surrounding such natural disasters as hurricanes, tornados, and earthquakes. The importance of the teacher's role in providing a stable routine, normalizing reactions, and helping students gain an intellectual understanding of the incident was emphasized. It was also noted that schools have a unique opportunity after a natural disaster to foster the development of a helping spirit in their students.

CHAPTER 5

Children and Death

> Dealing with the . . . grief that follows a . . . loss may be the most painful and disturbing challenge of our lives.
>
> —Staudacher, 1994, p. 1

Students may encounter death in their personal lives; in their communities or schools; or at a national level, as with assassination or the New York World Trade Center disaster, for example. Whatever the source of the student's experience with death, he or she will experience it differently at different ages.

To be successful in helping their students cope with the deaths they encounter, teachers must be aware of developmental stages (as most teachers are) and their relation to the understanding of death (with which teachers may be less familiar). The child's experience of death may vary somewhat with intellectual ability and familial attitudes; however, for the most part, the child's cognitive stage provides a workable guideline for intervention and behavioral expectations.

It is believed that before the age of three most children do not comprehend the finality of death. They may perceive it as someone leaving and coming back. This is one reason why young children do not grieve in ways that most adults expect. For example, a toddler might not cry or show signs of abandonment, at least not initially, any more than she would if the lost loved one went to work or the store.

Between the ages of three and five, children begin to become aware of the attitudes shown toward death by those around them. They may perceive that others are sad and even feel that they should look or act sad, as well. They may make associations between injury and sickness and death but are unlikely to grasp the concept of their own death or fully comprehend that all living things die.

The lack of cognitive awareness associated with the young child's experience of death does not mean that she or he will not have reactions to the loss; however, these reactions are more likely to be clinging to adults, fears of the dark, or regression to earlier behaviors than they are to be the traditional grieving behaviors of their elders.

Between the ages of five and eleven, children become more aware of the inevitability of death. They begin to appropriately associate death with age and injury and may even want to learn more about what happens when a living thing dies. The older the children are, the more similarity their reactions will have to that of adults; however, the occurrence of these reactions, being quiet or tearful, for example, may alternate with challenging or regressive behaviors.

In the preteen and teen years, young people become increasingly aware of the ramifications of death and develop increased cognitive understanding of how and why people die. While teens do develop a cognitive awareness of the connection of death to injurious behaviors and the value of healthy living habits in avoiding or at least postponing death, they often do not have an emotional grasp of their own vulnerability to death. This is thought to be one reason why death of a peer is so difficult for teens. The teen years are also a developmental period when youth become increasingly aware of the ideal as opposed to the real in society. They may be drawn to causes intended to prevent death, such as efforts to address world hunger and peace movements. Teens also begin to develop philosophies of death that will assist them in coping with death-related events as adults.

DEVELOPMENTALLY APPROPRIATE INTERVENTIONS

Preschool to Primary Grades

Parents are less likely to consider such therapeutic interventions as individual therapy for their young children who have encountered death; therefore, for these children, the preschool or kindergarten teacher may be the only source of support outside the family. In fact, the young bereaved child's needs are such that a caring, familiar adult may be in the best position to provide appropriate intervention.

The first task of the preschool or kindergarten teacher in assisting a child who has experienced death is to recognize the behaviors that may be associated with loss at this age and be patient. These young children may want to spend more time sitting with or near the teacher, may not venture far from her on the playground, and may show jealousy toward other children who get the teacher's attention. Children who were taking off boots and coats independently may now request help. Those who worked independently may ask for assistance. There may be toilet accidents or thumb sucking.

This is not the time for the teacher to attempt to modify these behaviors or comment on the evident regression. The best course is to interpret the behaviors as indicators of what the child needs and provide the extra attention and support. Unless there are factors complicating the adjustment for the child or family, the bereavement-related behaviors should lessen in two to three months, maybe sooner. A dependable routine is also important for the young grieving child. Since death by its very nature is disruptive, especially for the child who has experienced a familial loss, the school may be the one stable, familiar environment.

The Whole-Class Experience

Occasionally the whole class will experience a loss. This might be the death of a peer, the class's own teacher, a school or community leader, or a national figure. A teacher working with a class of young children who have experienced a loss should take cues for intervention, in part, from the closeness of the relationship between the deceased individual and the members of the class.

The death of the class's own teacher will obviously be handled differently from the death of a teacher in the school who was rarely or never encountered by the class. The nature of the death is also a factor, since natural deaths of older individuals are less likely to engender strong reactions from the community than, for example, a violent death on school grounds. These factors relate directly to the amount of class time the teacher should spend on the issue. The less connection the class has had with the deceased, the less attention the event should receive. Teachers of young children should not emphasize or call attention to a death event that is relatively remote to most of the children.

Young children tend to be less interested in details of a death, whether it was a suicide, for example, or whether it was a family member who killed the individual. They will, however, be subject to the emotional environment of the community and may be affected by its intensity. Drawing and play can provide an outlet for young children.

Another classwide alternative for a class of young students is a book about loss that can be read to the class and discussed. This is a less direct but effective technique for getting children to express their feelings about death. This indirect method is often more comfortable for teachers because they have more control over the activity and discussion. Another helpful activity is making a card or book for the family of the deceased.

Intermediate Grades

The primary difference between young children and those in intermediate grades, with regard to any intervention, is the readiness of the child to engage in discussion as a form of expression. Any adult who has asked a 10-year-old boy about his day and has just heard "fine" may question the wisdom of the writer in making this statement. While direct questioning at a time chosen by an adult may be less than productive, children in the intermediate grades do have the capacity to identify and express their feelings; however, having the ability to converse is not the same as being aware that it is helpful, as experience with many adults will also demonstrate.

Intermediate-age children will often express most when they do not feel that they are the central focus of inquiry. For parents, this means that casual conversations in the car or while cleaning up the yard can be the most productive. For the teacher, it means accompanying verbal expression with such tasks as drawing or reading. With intermediate-grade children, the discussion about the activity, along with personal reactions (if given voluntarily) can be the most important part of the intervention.

The Whole Class Experience

When the whole intermediate level class has experienced a loss, the teacher should provide accurate but limited information about the death. Rumors can run rampant among children of this age, and these rumors can take on gruesome tones. For example, in one experience of this writer, the children spread misinformation that their classmate had died at school. In reality, the child had become ill at school and died at the hospital. As a result of this misinformation, students were peeking into the classroom to see exactly where the child had died.

It is also important to remember that too much detail is unnecessary and can be overwhelming. In another instance with which the writer is familiar, teachers were reportedly advised by a mental health professional to inform the students that the death of a teacher's spouse was a suicide. This is more information than necessary about the death of someone the students did not even know.

At this developmental stage, children are unlikely to avoid the more controversial and sensitive topics death can bring to mind. The teacher should expect that issues regarding where we go when we die, whether the deceased is in heaven, whether she will be buried, what a coffin looks like, and stories of past deaths the child has encountered may come up. Teachers should avoid feeling the need to address these topics or provide answers to the pressing questions that will undoubtedly emerge. The effective part of the interaction is for students to have an understanding of the event at their developmental level and feel the support of one another. Comments that different people have different beliefs, admission that you don't know an answer to a question, or a simple "thank you for sharing" is usually sufficient.

Finally, such class projects as making cards, writing best memories, collecting money for flowers, or drawing pictures focus feeling and bring closure to the discussion.

Secondary Grades

Characteristics of most middle, junior high, and high schools complicate teacher intervention when a death occurs. Because there are so many teachers for any one student and daily schedules are less flexible, planning should be done in advance to determine which teachers will be most directly involved with the students when a death occurs. Usually a teacher who sees the class most frequently is the best individual to address the needs of the students. This will often be a homeroom or language arts teacher. Due to the nature of the subject, teachers in the language arts are usually in a good position to facilitate writing or speaking as a form of expression for the students. They are likely to be more comfortable with the process of class discussion about a wide range of issues because of their experience in teaching literature.

Subject area should never take precedence over strength in interaction with students when an intervener is chosen. In some circumstances, the choice of intervener will be obvious, such as a coach talking with his students when a member of the team dies; however, no educator should ever be coerced into working with the students around a crisis event.

Because of their developmental level, adolescents are in some ways easier and in some ways more challenging to assist when a death occurs than are younger children. The teen's ability to use and understand language offers teachers the advantage of engaging in a form of communication with which they themselves are comfortable. While one must find ways to get younger children to express their feelings, adolescents are more likely to express their sentiments, although not necessarily in a formal setting.

One must also remember that because teens are often emotionally labile, in sync with one another, and at a stage of development where they are particularly sensitive to issues of life and death, overreaction and contagion can occur if crises are handled inappropriately. The following are some general guidelines for schools to use in assisting adolescents when a school-related death occurs. Teachers do not always have the opportunity to influence policy. When they do, or when they are called upon to make decisions regarding how to address their own class, they should keep the following factors in mind:

- Inform students of the death or circumstances of the death in small groups, that is, in groups no larger than a traditional class size. Do not bring large groups of students together in an auditorium or cafeteria, for example. Inform students of the death in person. Do not use a public address system. Usually the classroom teacher is the best one to do this, unless the teacher is too emotionally involved with the loss or would prefer not to talk to the class.

- Provide accurate information to the extent that it is known to limit rumors. If some information is unknown or is confidential at the family's request, the teacher should admit to not having the information or say it is confidential.
- Be aware that students will be differentially affected. Consider the relationship of each student in the class to the deceased, and plan interventions accordingly. Close friends of the deceased are likely to need more support than those who hardly knew the student.
- Allow students to self-select if they need support outside of the classroom, for example, meeting with a guidance counselor, school psychologist, or other mental health professional brought to the school to assist the students. *But,*
- Notify support personnel of students most likely to be at risk due to prior losses, closeness to the deceased, or emotional factors.
- Maintain a flexible classroom routine.

Sometimes teachers are uncertain about the degree to which they should modify classroom activity. This is a matter of judgment, and it is difficult to make a recommendation that will apply to every situation. Generally, it is best to avoid tests and student presentations on the day the event is announced. Time should be taken to discuss the event, of course, if you are the teacher assigned to hold the discussion. If the discussion has taken place in another class, a comment regarding the loss should be sufficient, along with the change in class requirements you plan to make for that day and perhaps the next. Otherwise, the work of the day should be carried out.

Those who need to be excused to access schoolwide supports should be able to do so without too much attention being given to their absence or return. Two extremes of classroom management should be avoided. One is "work is the best therapy," which says if we pay attention to the loss we will just create problems, and "life must go on." The other is the constant emersion in the loss and repeated discussion in every class. This creates an emotional drain on all participants and can contribute to emotional overreaction in students who otherwise would have maintained some distance from the loss.

IF THE DECEASED WAS A PEER

One of the most difficult losses a class can experience is the death of a class member. Accurate information is especially important in this event because of the fear that the death of a peer can generate. Children should be informed that the death of a young person is very rare. If the student had an illness, the fact that the illness is uncommon should be shared with the class. If the classmate died in a car accident or fire, actual statistics on how rare this is should be mentioned.

The teacher should be willing to answer questions and allow students to talk about their classmate, including special memories, if they express an interest in doing so. This should not be done in a one at a time manner, since not everyone will want to speak. Keep in mind that students who were closest to the deceased may need special assistance.

Another challenging issue is what to do with the things of the deceased student. Teachers should avoid the impulse to remove all reminders of the deceased child. Generally, such personal items as a jacket, lunch box, and papers on top of the desk should be removed quickly; however, one should not be so quick to remove the desk and chair. It is best to give the class time to grieve. Removing things too quickly suggests that the students should just "get over it." Such an approach hinders necessary grieving and can shut down communication. The deceased child's work on a bulletin board need not be removed at all since all of the assignments will eventually come down anyway.

IF THE DECEASED WAS THE CHILD'S TEACHER

This is probably the most difficult circumstance of all school-related deaths for any elementary school child. When a peer dies, at least there is still an adult at school to guide and care for the child. The teacher maintains the reliable and supportive environment in spite of other losses. When the teacher is the one lost, the entire class must be considered to be at risk, at least in the short term. The later in the year that the loss has taken place, the harder it is likely to be on the child.

The loss of the teacher is further complicated by the impact of the death on the other adults in the school environment. In one situation of this type encountered by the writer, the other teachers found out about the death only moments before the beginning the school day, and some were not able to meet their own classes, let alone provide support to the class of the deceased teacher. In this circumstance, prior planning can mean the difference between managing or escalating a crisis. (See also chapter 11, "Crisis Response Teams.")

Reality Check

Early on a Tuesday morning, at the beginning of February, Mr. Jong, a fourth grade teacher at Greensville Elementary, died suddenly of a heart attack. The school principal, Mrs. Kraft, was informed two hours before the first bus arrived at the school. Because the school was relatively small, Mrs. Kraft was able to personally notify the teachers of the death by phone and ask them to attend a faculty meeting as soon as they arrived at the school. From this personal contact, she also learned whether the teachers felt able to come to school that day. Knowing how important their presence would be to the students, all of the teachers decided to attend, but it was evident at the meeting that the day was going to be very difficult for them.

Mrs. Kraft considered getting a substitute teacher for Mr. Jong's class but decided instead that his students would be more comfortable with adults they knew. The school guidance counselor spent the day with the class, and the principal was in the classroom as much as she could be. Other teachers joined the class when their own classes had specials.

Members of the school district's crisis intervention team contacted parents and sent a letter home with information and some suggestions on how they might assist the children. They invited parents and children to a meeting with the school psychologist that evening for a discussion of children's reactions to death and to address parents' questions. During the calls, the team asked parents if there were any reasons why a particular child might be at more risk.

Individual crisis team members saw the students who seemed most upset or who had been noted to be at risk by the parents. Teachers who knew most about how Mr. Jong did things were a great help to those who worked with the class. Students also helped by relaying how things were done. This served as an additional way for them to remember Mr. Jong. A plan was formulated with the substitute teacher who was to arrive the next day, including ways to periodically address the death but move back into a dependable routine.

At the evening meeting, the children spent some time making cards for Mr. Jong's family while the parents met with the school psychologist. (Children who did not attend were given the opportunity to do this the next day, if they chose to do so.) Parents, children, the school principal, and the school psychologist ended the meeting with a moment of silence to think about all that Mr. Jong had done for the school.

IF THE DEATH WAS A SUICIDE

Issues of confidentiality, contagion, and general discomfort complicate the school's position when the death in question was a suicide. A general rule of thumb is to share with students only what is known to be accurate and common knowledge. Immediately following an event, rumors fly. Classroom discussions based on rumor are not only counterproductive, but they can leave the school open to legal action if harmful inaccuracies are spread by school personnel.

Mental health professionals stress the importance of sharing accurate information. This should not be interpreted as a call to provide every bit of information to students. Elementary school children, especially, are not likely to benefit from hearing specific details of a death. For preschool and primary-grade children, stipulating that the death was a suicide is not necessary. The point of accurate information is to dispel rumors and reduce anxiety. Enough information to accomplish that task should be sufficient for younger children.

If the cause of death is common knowledge, intermediate-grade children are likely to ask questions, and the teacher should be prepared to answer truthfully and accurately, without belaboring the issue of suicide. Brief and age-appropriate discussions on depression and suicide prevention might be carried out by guidance counselors or school psychologists some time during the week of the event. Otherwise, the process for addressing any death classwide should be carried out.

There are likely to be more questions at the secondary level, and teachers should be prepared to answer the inquiries, if the answers are known and are public knowledge. Wishes of the family must be honored with regard to how much is revealed. If all the teacher knows is what he has read in the newspaper or seen on television, he must be sure to let the students know of his source and the possibility for error.

Students should be given the opportunity to ask questions, and their questions should have accurate responses, to the degree that is possible. Since the risk of suicide contagion exists at this age, open communication is of utmost importance, in part because it will provide the teacher with the opportunity to gauge the reactions of the students.

Group discussion with teens should be factual and avoid the extremes of making negative judgments about the deceased, on the one hand, and romanticizing or idealizing the deceased, on the other. Both of these positions increase emotionalism and intensity of reaction among peers. To reduce the potential for contagion among teens after a suicide, Brock (2002) recommends avoiding sensationalism, glorification, vilification, and excessive detail. Screening students for the need for counseling is important at all ages, but especially with the secondary population.

THE RISKS OF SILENCE

With the best of intentions, some educators will argue that children should be protected from bad news, and if it must be shared, then parents should be the ones to do it. There may be some rare instances when children can be protected from the news. Say, for example, that a well-loved school principal retires and moves away from the district. The next year he dies of a heart attack. Do the classroom teachers in that elementary school have to announce to their classes that their old principal has died? It is difficult to see the mental health advantage to the children of addressing the issue at school. School personnel may want to inform parents in a home-school communication and leave the decision on whether to share up to them.

Let's consider another scenario. A teacher in the child's elementary school has died. The school administration decides not to share the information at school. Obviously, some people at the school know. Word begins to leak. False rumors spread about the nature of the death. On the way home from school, children hear more from other children. Some go home to empty houses having just heard the news. There are no caring adults around, and what they have heard may be inaccurate and scary. Now we have a recipe for poor adjustment, repression of feeling, and anxiety. The outcome for the children is likely to have been better if this incident had been handled carefully and professionally *at school.*

When possible, it is good if parents can be the ones to share the news with their children. In this writer's experience, many parents would prefer to do that; however, the facts of most crisis situations are such that the event happens at school and cannot be hidden from the children, or the event is of such magnitude that the children will hear of it and need support before they see their parents. That is the very nature of a crisis incident.

Additional research is needed to help us learn more about when, how, and what to share with children in crisis situations. We can, however, say with some confidence that attempts to keep crisis situations quiet are rarely likely to succeed and, when they don't, the children find out the information under less than supportive circumstances.

MEMORIALS AND OTHER FORMS OF RECOGNITION

The issue of memorials is complex for several reasons. First, it is fraught with cultural overlay. The way we mark death is quite different in different cultures and varies from family to family. It is difficult to find a way that will meet a wide variety of needs. Second, decisions about memorials are often made at times when we are overcome with emotion.

Memorials and other forms of marking death carry very practical implications for schools. Rather than rush into a decision about a memorial, it is best to wait and give it ample thought. It is important to consider the wishes of those involved, but also what is best for the school. If the death in question was a suicide, memorials that romanticize the death or require the whole school to pay homage can increase the chances for contagion.

Another issue to be considered is that most schools, although they serve the young, are still likely to experience several deaths over a period of years, sometimes several in one year. Placing pictures of deceased students in a hall, for example, can over the years lead to a hall full of the pictures of dead students. One must ask to what degree that contributes to the mental health of those who attend the school. Teachers should always check the school's crisis intervention plan and with the crisis intervention team for advice on recognition of a death. Other suggestions are as follows.

- Always make participation optional.
- Plan activities in times and places that do make them optional.
- Offer a variety of suggestions for marking the death so that students will have opportunity to select one that works best for them.
- Do not imply in what you say or by what you do that one form, attending a funeral, for example, is better than another, like, writing a note to the family of the deceased.
- Do not imply by what you say or what you do that emotionalism, like crying, for example, is better or worse than a lack of a show of emotion.
- Consider the wishes of the family of the deceased.

WHEN TO REFER

Teachers and parents often wonder when a child's death reaction should be considered beyond the norm. General guidelines can be divided into two categories, *risk factors* and *behavioral indications*. Risk factors are characteristics of the child or his experiences that make him vulnerable to loss. Children at risk should be carefully monitored after a death experience. Behavioral indicators are extreme or unusual behaviors for the age and cultural group, or for the child, that did not exist before the loss. Keep in mind that these behaviors need not be the traditional signs of depression, such as crying or withdrawal. They can be irritability, use of drugs or alcohol, regression, or anger. These indicators can suggest poor adjustment or complications in the grieving process.

Time is a key element in the assessment of grief reactions. According to the *Diagnostic and Statistical Manual of Mental Disorders* (2000) published by the American Psychiatric Association, grieving behavior that interferes with life routine two months after the loss is experienced is usually considered to warrant attention in the adult; however, this should not be considered a firm guideline under all circumstances.

Cultural factors can play an important role here. Some cultures consider the "moving on" often recommended in Anglo societies to be a sign of disrespect for a deceased family member. Children's grief reactions usually do not last as long as those of adults; however, they are likely to be strongly influenced by how the adults in their environment are coping. The following is a list of risk factors that can make a child vulnerable to a problematic adjustment after a loss:

- *Prior losses.* We indeed seem to have a limited fund of resources to deal with loss. Each additional loss awakens reactions to prior losses, and results can be cumulative. Children who have lost parents early in life are extremely vulnerable, perhaps in part for this reason. Therefore, a child who has lost a parent and then a classroom teacher is at greater risk for adjustment problems than one who has lost only a teacher. It must also be noted that loss can take many forms. A move, the death of a pet, or parental divorce are all forms of loss that can leave a child vulnerable to another.
- *Sensitive temperament.* There is increasing evidence that suggests we are born with different tendencies toward forms of emotional reactions and behaviors. These tendencies are thought to have a physiological base, at least to some extent. Indeed, infants as young as a few weeks have shown signs of temperaments that are consistent with their adult characteristics. Some temperaments are more reactive. Most teachers would have little trouble in identifying which of their students would fit into this category, given enough time with a class. These overly sensitive children may be at greater risk for difficulty when they experience a death.
- *Familial Circumstances.* Research is not sufficiently developed to allow definitive statements about which family circumstances might put a child at greatest risk for a strong death reaction; however, situations that tap resources of a family to the extent that the

child's needs cannot be addressed present more potential problems for the child. The child who has lost a parent and whose remaining parent is incapacitated by the loss is at greater risk, for example, than one whose parent is coping adequately. A child who experiences the death of a peer is at greater risk if she has just been placed in foster care than she would be if she had a successful and long-term living arrangement with her current foster family.

- *Physical and emotional proximity to the event.* As common sense would suggest, students who witness an event close up are more likely to experience a complicated reaction, as are those who were emotionally close to the victim. The child who saw someone shot on the playground is more at risk for a stress reaction than the child who heard about it. The child whose friend was shot is more likely to be at risk than students who did not know the victim.

WHAT TO SAY TO PARENTS

Parents who are stressed by a death in the family may ask the teacher for advice on how to help the child adjust and even whether the child should attend religious services related to the death. Teachers should avoid making these decisions for parents. In general, parents should be advised to follow their own religious or philosophical beliefs and be supported in their own ability to make decisions related to their child; however, as a professional familiar with children, in general, and any one student in her class, in particular, the teacher can share impressions of the child and knowledge about the common reactions of children the child's age. The following guidelines can be used to help teachers make parents aware, if asked:

- Involvement of the child in death-related rituals should accommodate the child's age and attention span. If a younger child is to attend a religious service, for example, provision should be made for the child to leave early or at least be taken from the room periodically.
- Young children may not cry or appear sad, and this should not be interpreted by adults as a lack of respect for the family member who has died.

- Young children do not have the capacity to imagine what death rituals will entail and, therefore, they cannot self-prepare. A trusted adult should explain what will happen, including what the child should do and whom he will be with and when.
- Adult sharing of emotion and understanding of the death, in an age appropriate manner, can help the child cope and should not be avoided in an attempt to shelter.
- A death ritual experience that stretches adults beyond their own endurance should be avoided as a first death ritual for children.

Teachers must be careful not to advise parents based on their own opinions or personal experiences. Research-based information is appropriate for sharing with parents; personal or culturally based opinions are not. For example, a common value of mainstream American culture is that work heals; therefore, many Americans might emphasize the importance of the child returning to school immediately after a death in the family. Other cultures, many Mediterranean groups, for example, might find it disrespectful to return to work or school too quickly. This is purely a matter of values. There is no evidence that a child is harmed by spending time at home with family following a death if the length of time is reasonable, if it does not negatively affect the child's education, and if the time is being spent grieving in a healthy manner supported by the child's culture.

SUMMARY

In this chapter, we reviewed child and youth reactions to death and appropriate interventions from a developmental perspective. We outlined methods of communicating with students about death, including the importance of informing them in small groups, providing accurate information, and dispelling rumors. The role of the teacher in referring those who need special support was stressed. Memorials and other forms of marking death, as well as ways to assist parents, were reviewed. The importance of cultural sensitivity and avoidance of personal bias in providing crisis support was a central theme.

CHAPTER 6

The Suicidal Student

> If we can understand those factors that contribute to children bouncing back, becoming hopeful and resilient, then we can develop and implement more effective interventions.
>
> —Brooks, 2002, p. 78

FREQUENCY AND PRECIPITATING EVENTS

Suicide is rare in youth before puberty; however, suicidal ideation, attempts, and even completions do occur in children. Gestures or attempts in young children are sometimes overlooked or underestimated because the child may not have the cognitive awareness to select a means considered lethal by adults. A child who attempts to strangle himself by tying a sheet to the backboard of his bed may not be seen as making a true suicide attempt, but such behavior could be a sign of significant depression and must be taken seriously.

Suicide is the third most common cause of death in the United States among those aged 15 to 24. (Accidents are first and homicide second.) The rate increased significantly between the 1970s and 1990s, declined from the 1990s to 2004, and then increased again between 2003 and 2004 for selected age groups (American Association of Suicidology, 2010).

To some, suicide is so unthinkable it is associated with only the most mentally ill among us. We tend to believe that someone that disturbed would be obvious to anyone. Contrary to popular opinion, students who commit suicide are rarely psychotic, that is, so disturbed as to be out of touch with reality. They are, however, often suffering from depression. Depression, coupled with stressful life occurrences, can become overwhelming to youth.

Pitcher and Poland (1992) note that the most common triggering events in youth suicide are "arguments with parents, the breakup of a romantic relationship, the loss of a loved one, and extreme humiliation" (p. 72). Suicide of a peer or history of parental suicide, especially in combination with any of the previously mentioned common factors, increases the risk. Trouble with a teacher, failing grades, and changes in schools are other factors that can place significant stress on our youth.

One theorist postulates that suicide evolves from lifetime exposure to various forms of violence, coupled with feelings of not belonging (Joiner, 2009). Both of these have relevance to what students experience in schools. Not belonging and being targets of bullying have emerged as issues in studies of school shooters. Indeed, students who engage in such forms of violence as fighting or carrying a weapon to school have been found to be at a higher risk for suicide (Nickerson and Slater, 2009).

COMMON MYTHS

The primary role of the teacher in suicide intervention is to detect the signs when possible and make an immediate referral to the school's mental health professional. Unfortunately, teachers can fall prey to misconceptions about youth suicide, or suicide in general, that can cloud their judgment and cause them to miss important cues. See table 6.1 for clarification of some of these myths.

SIGNS AND DEMOGRAPHIC CHARACTERISTICS

While the detection of suicidal ideation can be complex, there are significant risk factors of which the teacher should be aware. Students who have a relative or friend who has attempted suicide are at greater risk to be attempters themselves. For adolescents, the risk is higher shortly after the suicide of a peer, so-called copycat suicides, or cluster suicides.

Table 6.1. Suicide Myth versus Reality

Myth	Reality
Those who talk of suicide will never actually act on the threat.	What we say we will do is actually a good indicator of what we will do. People who threaten suicide can and do take their lives. Threatening suicide is a very strong indicator of risk.
Students threaten suicide for attention. If we provide the attention, they will be rewarded for their behavior and threaten more often.	Students may threaten suicide for attention. These threats, however, can still lead to attempts. Students will not kill themselves because their suicidal ideas or behavior is appropriately addressed. They may kill themselves if it is not.
Students who are sociable and friendly will not attempt to take their lives.	While it is true that isolated students are more at risk, being sociable and having friends does not prevent a student from attempting suicide.
Students who are depressed/suicidal just need someone to talk to. If they can express their feelings, they will not act on suicidal thoughts.	Having someone to talk to is certainly better than having no one; however, just talking to a nonprofessional is not enough to address the needs of a suicidal student.
Students depressed enough to commit suicide will look sad and dejected or will cry.	Depressed children and adolescents do not necessarily show characteristics that adults might associate with sadness. Anger, irritability, and lack of motivation can also be indicators of depression or suicidal thoughts.
Nothing can really be done to prevent suicide. Those who really want to will find a way.	Suicidal feelings are rarely chronic. Appropriate treatment has a substantial likelihood of being successful.

Suicidal students may give away prized objects or talk of revenge, of how someone will be sorry, or of how others are better off without them. Language arts teachers may see repetitive themes of loss or death in writing; journal entries that emphasize loss, loneliness, or isolation; or writing that romanticizes death or suicide.

Demographic characteristics are not very helpful in determining risk for any one individual; however, they may help teachers assess the likelihood of facing a suicide crisis in their school setting, depending on the groups with which they most often work. For example, Native American boys are a higher-risk population for suicide (Poland and Lieberman, 2002). African American students have traditionally had lower rates of suicide than whites, but the difference has lessened in the last few years, with African American males showing a substantial increase.

Girls are much more likely to think about and attempt suicide than boys. Boys, however, are much more likely to die in an attempt. Causes for this are uncertain, but these statistics also hold true for adults. One reason sometimes given is the availability and attraction of more lethal means of suicide attempts for males, for example, firearms, as opposed to the means that may be chosen by females, for example, pills. Suicide with pills is complicated and requires awareness of dosage, timing, and physiological reactions. The use of a firearm is obviously simpler and faster. Availability of firearms in the environment substantially increases the risk of completed suicide for those of all ages (Poland and Lieberman, 2002). Most adolescent suicides occur at home.

Because drugs and alcohol reduce the youth's capacity to perceive accurately and think clearly, their use decreases the ability to problem solve. Students who abuse substances must be considered at higher risk for suicide, as well as other forms of self-harm. Substance abuse can also lead to depression, feelings of panic, fear, or paranoia, all of which can lead to transient, but nevertheless deadly, attempts to stop the pain.

PILING UP AND PILING ON

Suicidal ideation in youth that is not a result of substance abuse or psychosis (mental illness characterized by delusion or hallucination) often coincides with feelings of hopelessness, a sense that there is no positive way out of a dilemma, or a way to ease intense emotional discomfort. Sometimes this can be the result of one traumatic event, such as the loss of a relationship or the death of a significant other. More often it results from a series of events not always closely associated in time, although they may be. When these events, sometimes called *stressors*, accumulate, especially in a youth with few resources to draw upon and who is already depressed, risks for self-harm can increase.

One significant stressor is loss. Loss does not always mean a death or breaking of a personal connection. Losses can take many forms, including loss of self-esteem, loss of a privileged position, or loss of opportunity. Humiliation, shame, and guilt are all strong emotions that can result from loss. Change and failure are also significant stressors.

If stressors accumulate, the potential for negative effects is greater. A student who fails a course and experiences a breakup with his girlfriend is likely to be more at risk than the student who experiences only one of these events.

Clearly, not all youth who experience a piling up of stressors will be at risk for self-harm. Why not? We really don't know, but there is evidence that some characteristics of the environment and the individual can increase one's protection against a negative outcome. This ability to experience significant stress and still maintain one's equilibrium is known in the mental health literature as resilience. Three factors found to be associated with resilience in children are intellectual strength, positive relationships with adults, and temperament (Haggerty, Sherrod, Garmezy, and Rutter, 1994). Emery and Forehand (1994) further categorize the factors as individual, family, and extrafamilial. See table 6.2.

Table 6.2. Protective Factors Identified in Resilience Research

Individual Factors	Family Factors	Extrafamilial Support Factors
temperament (active, cuddly, good-natured)	warm, supportive parents	supportive network (e.g., grandparent, peers)
gender (being female prior to adolescence and male during adolescence)	good parent-child relations	successful school experiences
age (being younger)	parental harmony	
IQ		
self-efficacy		
social skills		
interpersonal awareness		
feelings of empathy		
internal locus of control		
humor		
attractiveness to others		

Source: Emery, R. E., and R. Forehand. (1994). Parental Divorce and Children's Well-Being: A Focus on Resilience. In R. J. Haggerty, L. R. Sherrod, N. Garmezy, and M. Rutter (Eds.), *Stress, Risk, and Resilience in Children and Adolescents* (p. 81). Cambridge, UK: Cambridge University Press. Reprinted with permission.

WHAT THE TEACHER SHOULD DO

The Individual Student at Risk

Teachers faced with a student they suspect is suicidal should trust their own judgment and request immediate consultation with a school mental health professional. It is not necessary for teachers to determine the student's exact intent before making a referral. Concern is sufficient reason to refer. In rare instances where the consultation cannot take place immediately, teachers should continue communicating with the student. The discussion is best initiated by an explanation of why you are concerned, for example, noting that the student seems preoccupied, unhappy, or distracted.

There are some guidelines the teacher can use to keep the interchange supportive but productive. It is important to *maintain a calm demeanor* to avoid frightening the student into wanting to avoid the interaction. *Maintenance of a nonjudgmental stance* is also a key to keeping communication open. If a student reveals suicidal thoughts to the teacher, such comments as, "Certainly you would never do such an awful thing," or, "That would be selfish," are unproductive and risk closing down the line of communication. Similarly, *it is not helpful to engage in confrontation or argue with the student* over the merits of the plan. Keep in mind that suicide is often a result of impulsivity, emotion, and a loss of perspective. For the teacher to respond emotionally or impulsively will only exacerbate the problem at hand.

Avoid the tendency to interrupt in an effort to talk the student out of the plan; however, the teacher should *guide the discussion* to keep it focused on important information he needs to gather, like whether the student actually has devised a plan or whether anyone else is involved (a suicide pact). If a student tells you she is thinking of suicide because her boyfriend has left her, for example, do not get sidetracked into talking about why he left or if he might come back. Those issues cannot be resolved quickly and should not be the focus during a crisis.

While you want to avoid an argument with the student over the merits of suicide, you also *should not sanction suicide as a viable option* no matter how difficult the student's situation may seem. One of the main goals of suicide intervention is to *help the person at risk see that there are other ways of solving the problem other than suicide.*

While the teacher cannot engage in treatment of suicidal ideation, it is reasonable to tell the student that other alternatives are certainly available even though the student may not be able to think of any at the moment. *Never tell a student that you do not believe he or she would really commit suicide or suggest that they are bluffing.* This could be interpreted as an invitation to prove oneself by making an attempt.

Students will sometimes ask the teacher to swear to secrecy before revealing any information. Since sincerity and trust are important to a helping relationship, and keeping a potential suicide a secret is out of the question, the teacher should explain that the goal is to keep the student safe and well, and that, as one who cares about the student, the teacher will do all she can to keep the student safe. At the same time, it should also be clear that every effort will be made to keep the details of the situation private, that is, that no one will be informed who does not need to know to help the student.

If you suspect a student is at risk, do not leave the student alone, even to call for assistance. Take the student with you to an appropriate office and have someone else stay with the student while you do what is required to get mental health support staff or administrators involved. The following are guidelines for appropriate teacher responses to the suicidal student:

- Do not keep threats or related comments secret.
- Contact mental health professionals and the school administration immediately. (The school's crisis intervention plan will usually determine whom the teacher is to contact, and that person will contact the others and the parents.)
- If a student mentions suicide, take it seriously and listen to him or her.
- Stay calm.
- Do not moralize or be judgmental.
- Avoid arguing or taking a confrontational stance.
- Do not leave the student alone.
- Do not sanction suicide as an option.
- Do not express disbelief or say that those who talk about suicide never do it.

Teachers should avoid attempts to counsel the suicidal student. Counseling under these circumstances is complex and should be left to a mental health professional. Well-meaning educators can actually play a role in limiting the student's motivation for professional counseling by attempting to meet the student's needs themselves. Students can become dependent on the teacher and even come to believe that talking to the teacher is all they need. Of course, this is not to suggest that the teacher should abandon or refuse to talk to a depressed or suicidal student, but the teacher's goal should be to get the student the required mental health services without delay. The teacher does not need the student's permission, or even parental permission, to refer an individual to the school's mental health professional.

As a trusted adult, a teacher can play a very important role in getting students to recognize the value or promise of mental health service. Teachers can tell whom the student will see, and, if they know the person, reveal a little about the mental health provider's personality or helpfulness. They can also make sure the student understands what will happen and when. All of this advance information is likely to reduce the student's anxiety and help her feel less alone, because she knows the teacher will guide her through the process.

In the unlikely event that the teacher receives contact by phone from a student who talks of self-harm, he should find out where the student is, the phone number of the location, and who else is present. The teacher should also ask if the student has already done anything to harm himself, such as taking pills. This information will be very important to interveners who have to call or locate the student. In a medical emergency, 911 should be contacted. Most communities also have mental health emergency numbers that can be located in the front of the local phone directory. Teachers should also always have after-hours numbers for their building principal and school mental health professional, usually the school psychologist.

It may be helpful for the teacher interacting with the suicidal student to know that whether the suicidal ideation is a result of a precipitating event, like a death or breakup, or part of a clinical depression, treatments available are often very effective. Hospitalization is not always warranted, and, with appropriate intervention, a change in mood can take place within days. Obviously, this is not the case in all situations and will be less likely if the student has made prior suicide attempts or has experienced emotional difficulties over an extended period of time; however, the potential success of treatment underscores the importance of detection and immediate action.

Reality Check

Mrs. Juarez teaches eighth grade English at Wallingboro Middle School. Joan Quints, who has been a motivated, if not stellar, student has not turned in her last two assignments. Mrs. Juarez asks Joan to stay after class so she can find out why the assignments have not been turned in.

When asked about the assignments, Joan just shrugs her shoulders and says she doesn't know why she didn't turn them in. Mrs. Juarez asks her if she is feeling okay, and Joan begins to cry. She says her parents are away. They have left her at home with her 10-year-old brother, who won't listen to anything she says. She has been kicked off the volleyball team for missing practice, and nothing is going right. She mentions that she is tired of trying and feels like giving up, especially since her boyfriend said he's sick of her being so down all the time.

Mrs. Juarez asks, "How do you mean, you feel like giving up?" Joan replies, "No one would miss me, except my parents would have to stay home and take care of my brother." "When you say no one would miss you, that makes me think you mean you wouldn't be around. Is that what you mean?" Mrs. Juarez asks. "Yes, I'd rather be dead than have all of these problems."

At this point, Mrs. Juarez knows she must treat Joan as a student who is potentially suicidal. She explains that she knows several ways to help. She also knows that she cannot send Joan home to an empty house and must work quickly to find support for Joan before the school day ends.

It is important to note that when Joan said she felt like giving up, Mrs. Juarez could simply have told Joan to keep trying and get her assignments in because a bad grade would only make things worse. By being willing to talk less, listen more, get into deeper issues, and probe just a bit, she learns some important things about Joan and prevents a serious problem from becoming a major crisis.

On the surface, the things Joan complains about could easily be dismissed as not worthy of her intense reaction. Joan offers another important lesson here. If a student is already depressed, issues that may seem minor can be precipitating factors for suicide. The wise teacher will never interpret what is going on with a student by looking at just the facts. It is not only what happens to us, but how we interpret what happens, that makes a difference. What others might consider only troublesome could be perceived as insurmountable to a depressed youth.

The Depressed or Suicidal Student in Therapy

Suicidal or depressed students who are in therapy with outside practitioners or agencies still come to school, and teachers continue to play important roles in their lives. Insight on how to play that role is available from Dr. Leston L. Havens, a professor of psychiatry at Harvard Medical School. His recommendations are intended for therapists in training. He suggests that they protect their client's self-esteem, offer understanding, provide a sense that a better future is possible, listen more, and talk less (1999). Although school is a different context, a good teacher can do the same.

Therapists outside of school often appreciate the input of classroom teachers because of the intimate daily view they have of children. Teachers can be the first to notice signs of improvement or relapse. The need to protect the privacy of the student and the family, however, is frequently an impediment to effective participation of teachers on the mental health team. Teachers who are privy to mental health treatment information can help create a positive image for all educators by recognizing how essential confidentiality is to a helping relationship. They can enhance their effectiveness and contribution to the well-being of students in therapy in the following ways:

- *Building strong professional relationships with the school psychologist, school counselor, and support teams.* These relationships enhance trust between professionals. It is important for both the teacher and the school mental health practitioner to know that information shared about a student will be handled capably and with sensitivity.

- *Informing parents of mental health support services available at the school and how to access them.* Teachers are the parents' guides to the education system. They are the first educators parents meet. They are the ones parents get to know and the easiest to access. Every teacher should know how to assist parents in getting the help they need. This involves a great deal more than simply providing a phone number or the name of the principal. It means assisting in navigating the system, providing descriptions of the types of service, and perhaps making the first contact with the provider. While some teachers may be unaware of the importance of confidentiality, others are so concerned about it that they fail to involve mental health service providers at the school when doing so could enhance the circumstances of the child. Sharing information with those in the school with a need to know to serve the child is not a breech of professional ethics. Failure to inform when service could have been enhanced or would have alerted the school mental health personnel to dangerous circumstances could be.
- *Facilitating communication between the school mental health providers, the parents, and the therapist or agency in the community serving the child.* Remember that formal written parent permission should always be obtained before teachers share information with an outside therapist or agency. An oral parent request is insufficient.
- *Documenting signs of improvement or regression in the student.* It is helpful for teachers to log important information about a student's progress so they do not forget about it at a later date.
- *Responding to requests for information from community agencies or therapists in a timely fashion once parent permission has been received.* Timing can be key when relaying information to prevent delay in treatment.
- *Refusing to share information about a student or family with anyone in the school who does not have a need to know.* Personal information about a student should only be shared with others who have a need to know to serve the child.
- *Cooperating with parent and therapist requests for modifications at school that are intended to help the child.* Refusing to utilize interventions suggested by the therapist because they are inconvenient

is hardly cooperative or helpful; however, teachers who have questions about the advisability of an intervention recommended by an outside service provider should check with the school mental health practitioners or building support team.

• *Taking action immediately if signs of suicide or serious depression resurface.* Again, teachers can be the first to notice signs of improvement or relapse, and it is important that a relapse is addressed in a prompt manner.

The General Population of Students

Suicide is rarely mentioned in books, on television programs, or in movies appropriate for children; however, the issue may be present in teen literature or programming. In any general population of teens, there are likely to be some who experience suicidal ideation or have even attempted suicide. There may be others in treatment for depression or going through trying circumstances.

There is no way for the teacher to know to what degree these situations are present in any classroom. For that reason, given the contagion issues surrounding suicide, it is best to avoid literature and film in your classroom that feature suicide as a central theme. If such material is already part of the curriculum, steps should be taken in advance to prepare for potential reactions. Such preparation might include sending letters home to parents letting them know that the topic will come up in upcoming lessons. Parents can then notify school mental health personnel if they think their child would be placed at risk, or they can be given the option of not having their child participate in the lesson or program. Procedures for self- or teacher referral to mental health support personnel at school should be in place.

When exposure to such themes is out of the control of the school, if a television program involving suicide (especially teen suicide) has been aired, for example, schools should offer support and counseling to students who might be at risk or who found the program troublesome. Teachers should give thought to those students in their classes who might be placed at risk from exposure to such material.

Some schools have adopted schoolwide suicide prevention programs. While one might assume that these programs would be beneficial, results regarding their effectiveness have been mixed, suggesting that they should be used with caution (Dorwart and Ostacher, 1999). Some programs have had positive results. The most successful programs target those at risk, have an efficient referral process in place, and train a wide range of school personnel (Kalafat and Lazarus, 2002).

The National Association of School Psychologists and the National Association of Secondary School Principals support the use of SOS (Signs of Suicide), a screening program for secondary students that includes an educational component about suicide and related issues (Poland and Lieberman, 2004). The program offers instruction for high school students on reacting to suicide as a health emergency and recognizing signs of suicide and depression in themselves and others. The school staff is also trained. A packet with a screening tool, brochures, and an educational video is also provided to the school (Screening for Mental Health, Inc., 2010).

One study found that exposure to the SOS program significantly increased the number of high school students seeking help for emotional problems at school (Aseltine, 2003). Others found that those who experienced the program were less likely to report having made a suicide attempt (Aseltine and DeMartino, 2004; Aseltine, James, Schilling, and Glanovsky, 2007). Given the sensitivity and complexity of this topic, teachers should not provide suicide education independently in their classrooms unless it is part of a systemwide approved program, and even then it should be done with the necessary mental health professional supports in place.

Federal and state legislation encourages, and in some instances requires, the development of suicide prevention programs in schools. For a description of the Youth Suicide Early Intervention and Prevention Expansion Act of 2004 and the Garret Lee Smith Memorial Act, as well as laws enacted in your state, go to www2a.cdc.gov/phlp/suicide legislation.asp.

SUMMARY

In this chapter, we addressed the teacher's role in suicide prevention. Myths surrounding suicide can prevent teachers from playing their most important role, which is the detection and support of children and adolescents suffering from depression or experiencing severe stress. Effective relationships with mental health providers inside and outside of the school enhance the teacher's opportunity to help students cope. Because treatment for depression is likely to be successful in preventing suicide, it is essential that teachers be willing to make referrals to mental health professionals and that they assist therapists in monitoring the progress of students in treatment.

CHAPTER 7

The Hostile/Aggressive Student

> How children choose solutions available to them appears to be as-
> sociated, in part, with how they perceive the motivation of others.
>
> —Aberson and Shure, 2002, p. 112

Throughout this book, an attempt has been made to address the issue of crisis realistically and without overreaction. This is especially important because so many of the readers will be teachers in training who are not yet aware of the degree to which the school environment will place them at risk. Most teachers are never assaulted or even threatened. Many of the hostile and aggressive acts that do take place could have been avoided had the teacher been better prepared to cope with the situations that did arise.

Often hostile interactions of any kind are a result of a series of actions and reactions that escalate. Stop the interchange at any point in the series and you avoid the heightened emotion and thus the risk. One just has to think of any altercation in one's life, in school, or at home, and it is possible to, in hindsight, see where things might have been stopped or at least cooled.

For example, a child in an elementary school was involved in a fight in which he was clearly the aggressor. The child had been in several fights before, and the principal was ready to put a stop to this behavior. She decided to suspend the student and called the child's mother to come to pick him up at school. After being asked to wait for several minutes before seeing the principal, the mother was eventually asked into her office.

Although the parent was obviously quite angry, and even before both were seated, the principal described the child's behavior and her own dissatisfaction with it in some detail. The mother interrupted in a raised voice, blaming the school. The principal, also in a loud manner, commented that the mother was responsible for the child's behavior, at which point the mother hit the principal and shoved her into a bookshelf nearby. The principal was bruised but not seriously harmed.

Looking back at this instance, one can see several points where the situation could have been calmed. First, the longer the mother waited, the more frustrated and angry she was likely to become. Having her wait could have contributed to the problem. Second, a heated discussion is more likely to escalate with both parties standing than if they are seated. Third, a parent who was obviously already angry was probably not ready to accept blame for her child's behavior, at least not at that moment. Finally, if the principal had addressed the student's behavior sooner, before she became "fed up," she might have been able to deal with the mother more carefully. The intention is, of course, not to excuse the assaultive behavior, but to consider ways of planning for, and perhaps preventing, such incidents.

PICKING UP ON SIGNS AND GIVING SIGNALS

How do you know when someone is angry? We have all argued with someone at one time or another. What does that person look like when angry with you, or at least when they are ready to take it out on you? There will be signs of tension. These signs can be in such facial expressions as glaring or frowning. They can be demonstrated by a confrontational stance, pacing, or hand twitching. If the individual is larger than you are, he or she may loom over you.

The biggest mistake we can make as professional educators when confronted with an angry individual is to do what comes naturally. When we are confronted, the natural chemical reaction of the body is to prepare to fight. While few teachers would entertain the possibility of fighting with a student, our natural reactions can lead to raised voices, a posture that suggests squaring off, and other signs of heightened emotion. These natural reactions further escalate the conflict, can threaten or humiliate the student, and can develop into power plays that someone has to lose.

Unfortunately, some educators see a student's anger as a personal affront and representation of a lack of respect for them as individuals. They feel the need to address every negative comment and every slump in the chair as though they will lose all authority if they let it pass unnoticed. This reaction makes it more difficult to maintain composure and focus on the problem at hand, because the teacher becomes personally and emotionally invested in making the student behave in a certain way.

Students bring their worlds with them to school. They bring their reactions to their morning class to your afternoon class, and they bring social frustrations to biology. The emotional reactions they bring are just one more fact of life in schools and are best addressed as problems to be solved, not altercations to be won. Maybe when a teacher leaves an obviously angry student alone for the moment, he is not saying you win, but rather I understand enough about human nature to know when to back off. So, one of the first decisions a teacher must make in crisis intervention is whether to do something about a certain behavior.

Behaviors that are potentially harmful or that interfere with teaching will have to be addressed at the moment. Annoying or disrespectful behaviors, especially if demonstrated by students who are very emotional (based on history or current signs), are best addressed outside of class. If a student wants to sulk at the back of the room or chooses not to participate on a given day, let it go, wait to see if there is a pattern, and plan a way to address it outside of class, perhaps with the aid of school mental health support staff.

Students under the influence of drugs or alcohol give another kind of message that teachers must heed. Awkward gait, slurred speech, dilated pupils, and certain odors are all signs that students may be under the influence. You should know these signs, because these students may have less ability to control their behavior. They may act in ways that are uncharacteristic of them, which can catch the teacher off guard. Teachers should also be alert to signs that a student may have a weapon, for example, hands in pockets or under jackets.

Holding Steady

Sometimes students show more than irritation and may actually be close to losing control. In those situations, you will be glad that you engaged in some advance planning. Knowledge of a plan helps the teacher feel confident and in control. Rehearsal of procedures and techniques leads to a degree of overlearning that makes behavior nearly automatic, even under stress. Since so many different scenarios are possible, there are no foolproof ways to handle the angry, nearly out-of-control, or out-of-control student; however, some of the most common recommendations in the crisis intervention literature include the following:

- Speak in a calm clear voice at a medium tempo and loudness.
- Move to a location where both parties can be seated, unless the location would be unsafe.
- Do not "square off." Stand slightly to the side of the student.
- Move to a location where there is no audience, unless the location would be unsafe, or remove the audience.
- Do not finger point or use confrontational gestures.
- Do not argue or defend your point of view.
- Give the student the opportunity to briefly explain his feelings and the cause of the problem.
- State your requests and the outcomes of compliance or noncompliance.
- Offer the student options for resolution of the disagreement, all of which are possible from the school's point of view. (These may have to be only temporary until more attention can be given to the matter.)
- Offer to help the student address the problem at hand, if possible.

Do not do the following:

- threaten the student
- make jokes
- insist on any one behavior as the only way the situation can be resolved

- make negative statements about the student
- suggest that the student is bluffing and will not carry out the threats

While it may seem that a gentle pat or touch on the shoulder would serve to calm a student who is upset, physical contact can be easily misinterpreted under stressful circumstances and should be avoided. It is better to give the individual some space and refrain from touching. The Crisis Prevention Institute recommends one-and-a-half to three feet of distance but notes that this is not the same for all individuals. The more upset an individual appears to be, the more important appropriate distance becomes (Crisis Prevention Institute, 2005). Several sources offering recommendations to teachers on intervention once a student is out of control note that higher levels of emotion and acting out will be followed by lower levels and that teachers should try to communicate with students when they are at lower levels (Callahan, 1998; Crisis Prevention Institute, 2005).

In the event of a true potential threat of violence, you will be pleased that you have planned ahead with regard to colleague communication and the physical layout of your classroom. These and other ways to prepare are discussed in the prevention section of this book.

Reality Check

The last bell of the day has rung at Waterford High School. Mrs. Conte is seated at her desk cleaning up and preparing to leave when Roy, a student in her senior English class, comes to the door. He storms into the room claiming in a loud voice that this damn school has done it again and that Mrs. Conte has cheated him out of the grade he deserved on his midterm project. He says this whole school and the class suck. Roy is generally a weak student who has had past altercations with other students. This is the first time he has ever angrily confronted a teacher.

Mrs. Conte rises and moves slowly toward the door. Moving closer to Roy, but not too close, she pulls out a chair near to the door and asks him to sit. He moves around the room a bit, flailing his arms and saying he doesn't want to sit. He's pissed off and wants his grade changed. In a calm but clear voice and looking directly at Roy, Mrs. Conte tells

Roy that she is willing to discuss his grade but will not do so if he continues to use language unacceptable in school. She says that she has 10 minutes to talk with him if he would like to sit. He angrily pulls at the chair and sits with arms crossed. Mrs. Conte says she will give him a minute to clear his head before they begin their discussion because she has to make a phone call.

Without leaving the room, Mrs. Conte calls a colleague, saying that she will be ready in 10 minutes and he should not leave without her, and, yes, he should just meet her outside of her classroom. Sitting down with Roy, she explains that she will take notes on his concerns, review his work, and meet with him in the next day or two. Roy voices his complaints. Mrs. Conte takes notes and in 10 minutes she ends the meeting by telling Roy that she will get a note to him when she has reviewed everything, and they can talk again.

Let's review Mrs. Conte's behavior and the reasoning behind what she has done. Although she was seated when first confronted, Mrs. Conte gets up and moves to the door. She does this because she does not want to have an angry student between her and the exit. She moves deliberately, but not quickly, to avoid startling the student or giving him the impression that she is frightened.

She sets clear rules with regard to her willingness to discuss his problem and speaks directly to him. The message is that, if he is nearly out of control, she is capable of setting limitations. Her verbal communication must be simplistic because, in Roy's emotional state, he can misinterpret or miss the point of the message altogether.

Mrs. Conte's phone call is to a colleague with whom she has made a prior arrangement regarding the unlikely event of interaction with a student during which she feels threatened. Her colleague knows that should she call and speak as though he is waiting for her, he should come to her class and check on things. The call also gives Roy a minute to calm down.

Mrs. Conte should not make any comments about the grade at that time. Should she decide to change it, it would appear she had been threatened into doing so. Should she decide not to, she would reignite the crisis situation she has worked so hard to manage.

Her next meeting with Roy should include a third party, perhaps the guidance counselor, and plans must be made to further assess the reasons for Roy's acting out behavior with other students and his teacher. He will be reminded that the language he used is unacceptable at school, and the need for an anger management intervention for Roy will be assessed.

Where were the mine fields here? What could Mrs. Conte have done that could have made matters worse? She could have told Roy in a raised voice to get out of her room and that she was not going to have any student talk to her that way. He might have left; however, he also might have taken his anger out on a peer or through an act against the school, for example, vandalism.

Mrs. Conte could have insisted that he go with her directly to the office because she was going to have him suspended for using such language. In all likelihood, he would have refused. How could she make him go? She couldn't.

She could have engaged in an hour of discussion and explanation about why she graded him as she did. This is much like arguing with the student and is fruitless when a student is emotionally upset. It also sends the message that the teacher is trying to convince the student she was correct in giving the grade. He is unlikely to agree, and his agreement is not a requirement of the grading system. Making notes signals Mrs. Conte's willingness to take his problem seriously and, of course, if she said she would review her grading of his work, she should do so.

THE ROLE OF THE AUDIENCE

The role of the audience in behavior management in schools is central and too often ignored. Since true crisis prevention requires an evaluation of the causes of negative behavior, understanding the role of the audience at all levels of behavior management is crucial. With almost all activity in schools taking place in groups, audiences are hard to avoid. Consider the following scenarios with regard to both the long-term and short-term effects of having an audience present.

* * *

Carol frequently comes to school without her homework. Each day when her teacher, Mr. Cranz, collects homework, he comments that

Carol does not have hers done. After this goes on for several days, he reprimands her again for not having her homework and tells her that he will be calling her parents that night.

* * *

Juan regularly comes in from recess with a complaint about one of his classmates, that they took his ball, that they wouldn't let him play with them, or that they broke the rules while playing a game, for example. His teacher, Mrs. Rome, believes he is beginning to become a "tattle-tale" and that this will have a negative effect on how the other children perceive him. The next time he has a complaint after recess, she reminds him that no one likes a "tattletale" and that he is going to have to learn to get along with everyone better or he will not have any friends.

* * *

Class has been dismissed and, as they walk out the door, Carol and Marie are having an argument because Carol told Marie's friends that Marie was trying to steal her boyfriend. Instead of leaving class, the other students are starting to gather around to listen to the girls argue. Anxious to end her day, Mrs. Clark urges the class and the girls out of her room.

* * *

Before we consider the impact of the audience in each of these instances, a brief review of the circumstances that put children at risk for emotional difficulty might be helpful. In prior chapters, humiliation, loss, and isolation were mentioned in various contexts as precipitating factors for negative emotional reactions in children. Humiliation, by its very nature, implies embarrassment in front of an audience.

Loss of respect or stature among peers, loss of reputation, and to some extent even loss of self-esteem are all significant forms of loss requiring an audience. Finally, isolation often results from loss of positive reputation or building of a negative reputation as a student who is always in trouble, not very capable, or just not liked by the teacher.

Mr. Cranz is engaging in a common behavior, which, on the surface, seems to be a requirement of his role. After all, students are supposed to do homework, and not addressing their failure to complete it might encourage maladaptive behavior. The issue here is not whether it should be mentioned at all, but whether is should be mentioned before an audience, the class.

If Carol is a good student who used to do her homework, there is some reason why it is not getting done now. Whatever that reason is, Carol is likely to feel partially exposed, because the teacher has addressed the issue before the class. If Carol is a weak student who has rarely done her homework, her weaknesses have now been emphasized before an audience. Whatever the root cause may be for the absent homework, Mr. Cranz has not addressed it. What he has likely done is create a negative feeling in Carol and has either tarnished her positive reputation with the class or enhanced a negative one.

Why not address the issue privately? A lack of time is sometimes given as a cause for the need to address issues during class. The cost in loss of positive student relations and negative effect on the student is not worth the time saved. The best alternative is a personal, face-to-face meeting. If time really will not allow such a meeting, why not write a note, send an e-mail, or even have several copies of a form that goes to students who are slacking off on homework completion?

Mrs. Rome has made some assumptions about the cause and effect of Juan's behavior. Assuming one knows the cause of a child's behavior with little or no investigation is risky, even if one is engaging the child privately. When the teacher shares these assumptions with the class, she could unknowingly be laying the foundation for a crisis.

Mrs. Rome has assumed that Juan is a "tattletale" without looking into the possibility that he is being bullied. In fact, the nature of his complaints is not uncommon among students who are bullied. If bullying is the issue, by making her comments in front of the class, Mrs. Rome is not only failing to address the problem, she is participating in the bullying. She is also likely to be increasing Juan's frustration, since he has been unsuccessful in getting her to intervene on his behalf.

Whether Juan needs to develop better social skills or he is being bullied, or both, this situation warrants further investigation. A playground observation and private conversation with each of the students involved would probably shed a great deal of light on the nature of these circumstances; however, if Mrs. Rome believes that she does not have the time or skill to address the issue (of course, the point of this book is that teachers can develop these skills), she should make a referral to a mental health professional in the school.

Mrs. Clark is missing a prime opportunity to prevent a crisis. Because reputations among peers are so important, especially to teens, fights might actually take place between reluctant parties, once their reputations are believed to be at stake. All Mrs. Clark did was remove the potential fight and its audience to a location where it might be more likely to take place. Letting the rest of the class leave and giving the girls the opportunity to discuss the issue with an adult present is likely to have been more productive.

Given the realities of a busy teacher's life, it would also have been appropriate, if necessary, to make an appointment to meet with the girls at another time or make an appointment for the girls with the school's mental health professional. In either case, the girls should be placed on their honor to wait to discuss this issue when it can be given careful attention. This approach recognizes the importance the participants may place on the topic, even if the teacher does not share their opinion. It offers an "out" to whichever of the parties might be less willing to fight and takes away the impulse of the moment so important to aggressive interactions. The teacher's effort may not be successful and the fight may take place anyway; however, a well-planned intervention offers some chance of avoiding a potentially dangerous situation.

Another example of how the use of an audience can create problems is when teachers write the names of misbehaving students on the board. The teacher is focusing the attention of the audience on the misbehaving child (which can reinforce negative behavior) and is announcing to the audience which students are out of favor. This is enhancing a reputation, but not a positive one.

What possible benefit can there be to the teacher, the misbehaving student, or the class for publicly labeling a student and, therefore, bolstering his identity as a "problem?" The wise teacher will be sensitive to the impact of the audience on any school activity or event and will plan to use that impact for the benefit of the students and the school.

AGGRESSION AGAINST PEERS

Aggression in schools can take many forms. Some of it is organized, for example, when community gang violence moves into the school. Some of it is spontaneous and takes place between peers who seem fairly evenly matched, and some takes the form of aggression against a victim or one who cannot or does not respond with at least a fairly equal form of aggression.

Preventing and coping with gang violence is beyond the scope of this book. While gang violence can certainly result in traumatic experiences for students at school, incidences of gang violence rarely have their roots in the school itself. Teachers in schools where gang violence is an issue should be aware of the intervention programs available in the community and be well versed in the school's plan for collaboration with these programs.

Suggestions for intervention to prevent aggression between peers are similar to those for teachers confronting an angry student. Being alert and aware of which students seem most prone to violence or aggression is a good approach, but this is not foolproof. Detecting rumblings of coming trouble is a little easier if the teacher spends time with students and is observant. When that also fails, as it sometimes does, preventing the escalation of a conflict is of the utmost importance. To do this, teachers must be willing and able to engage in some conflict resolution with students, before emotions are running too high for attempts to be successful.

There are several ground rules that are helpful. These directives are to be set by the teacher and are not intended to be "negotiated."

- Both parties must agree to give discussion a chance.
- Both parties must agree to listen to each other and the teacher.
- Both parties must agree to state their point of view.

The presence of a third party, the teacher, who is not biased and does not engage in emotionalism will often have a calming effect; however, it is also important for the teacher to remember that she represents the school and must periodically make the school's position clear regarding consequences should school policy or rules be breached.

Sometimes students who are reluctant to engage in hostile acts can use the consequences as face-saving excuses to avoid confrontation and, of course, that is one of the purposes of such consequences. Whatever system of conflict resolution one uses, and there are several, the most important part of the process is to get the parties to think rather than act impulsively. The intent is to get students thinking about the reasons for and consequences of their actions.

Conflict resolution programs that involve peer facilitators provide the important element of a model like oneself who has used the process successfully. For an excellent and concise review of peer mediation and conflict resolution techniques, see Myrick's (2002) chapter in *Best Practices in School Crisis Prevention and Intervention*.

Sometimes the educator will come upon a fight already taking place. The Crisis Prevention Institute (1994) has produced a series of DVDs designed to help educators cope with hostile/aggressive students, one of which addresses intervening in fights at school (*Nonviolent Crisis Intervention for the Educator: Fights at School*). The presenters emphasize the importance of avoiding risk to the participating students, as well as the teacher. To that end, teachers are advised to get assistance, avoid getting in the middle of a fight, and remove the audience. Follow-up that leads to some resolution of the incident is strongly recommended and is considered essential for preventing crises in the future. Other recommendations that appear in the literature on student fights include getting the students' attention with a loud command or noise, telling them to stop, using their names, and giving clear verbal commands (Fields, 2002).

The Crisis Prevention Institute offers training in physical forms of crisis intervention that are to be used only as a last resort. Teachers who are in high-risk situations should seriously consider nonviolent physical crisis intervention training. Because the use of physical techniques requires careful instruction and monitoring, suggestions on physical crisis intervention cannot be made responsibly in solely written material and will not be addressed here. The Crisis Prevention Institute training is offered on-site at schools and at sites across the country. A "training of trainers" is also offered, allowing schools to send one person for extensive training who can then teach others (see appendix B).

BULLYING AND OSTRACISM

Not very long ago, books on childrearing and classroom management emphasized the need for social skill development in children who were bullied. It was suggested that victims of bullies would have to learn these necessary skills or experience the negative consequences. Too much interference from adults, it was said, would prevent the children involved from working things out for themselves and learning from the experience.

Recent research on bullying and episodes of violence in the schools have led to different conclusions. Bullying creates anger and desire for revenge on the part of the victim. Following a study of 15 lethal student-on-student attacks that took place between 1995 and 2001, researchers concluded that retribution for teasing and ostracism was the primary motive in most of the incidents and that the treatment the killers had experienced was "relentless, humiliating, and cruel" (Leary, Kowalski, Smith, and Phillips, 2003, p. 212).

Victims are rarely successful in stopping the bullying on their own. Studies of victims have clearly indicated their desire for intervention from adults at school and have documented that bullying is not limited to dark corridors or hidden pathways home, but that it occurs in main halls and cafeterias of schools. While various curricula and intervention programs do exist, there is no substitute for the aware teacher who informs his students that intimidating behavior will not be tolerated.

In a review of the reactions of preservice teachers and children to a video portraying a teasing incident, researchers found the preservice teachers to significantly underestimate how upsetting teasing was to the children (Landau, Milich, Harris, and Larson, 2001). The authors expressed concern that adults may underestimate the negative impact being embarrassed in front of peers has on children. Other researchers have also noted that educators tend to overlook negative comments and name calling among peers (Espelage and Swearer, 2008).

Many schools have adopted antibullying programs. A 2006 study of a nationally representative sample of school districts found that 94.8% of them had antibullying policies in place. Sixty percent of the states were reported to have policies in 2007 (Jones, Fisher, Greene, Hertz, and Pritzl, 2007), and, in 2008, 33 states were reported to have antibullying laws (Swearer, Espelage, and Napolitano, 2009). For a thorough review of the legal issue and a look at legislation and policies state by state, see Swearer, Espelage, and Napolitano, *Bullying Prevention and Intervention: Realistic Strategies for Schools* (2009).

Antibullying programs take various forms and have not been fully researched; however, most are based on the wise premises that an effective program will target both the bully and the victim and that the most effective programs are schoolwide. Whether or not a schoolwide antibullying program exists in their school, teachers can create an atmosphere within any classroom that discourages such behavior. Class rules, role modeling, and instruction in problem solving can help reduce teasing and intimidation. When bullying does take place, the teacher should explain, in individual sessions with the bully, how the teacher perceives the behavior, why it cannot be permitted, and what consequences are likely to follow if it is not stopped. Immediate follow-up to find out if the bullying has ceased underscores the importance the teacher places on ending the behavior.

The Olweus Bullying Prevention Program is a well-known program intended to operate schoolwide and even extend to members of the community. (For a detailed description, see Olweus et al., *Olweus Bullying Prevention Program Training Manual* [2003], listed in appendix B.) The program includes administration of an anonymous questionnaire to students on the extent of the bullying problem, development of schoolwide rules against bullying with consequences, and teacher attention to locations in the school where bullying is most likely to take place.

The most important part of the process is the development of a school climate that attends to and discourages bullying, while fostering positive problem-solving behavior. Some key features of the program that teachers can use with individual students include meetings with victims to provide support, gather information, and develop plans; meetings with bullies to inform of and administer consequences and monitor the bully's behavior; meetings with parents of both parties; and referral to mental health professionals for both parties, as needed (Limber, 2004).

Another schoolwide antibullying program with which teachers should be familiar is Bully Busters. (For a detailed description, see

Horne, Bartolomucci, and Newman-Carlson, *Bully Busters: A Teacher's Manual for Helping Bullies, Victims, and Bystanders (Grades K–5)* [2003], listed in appendix B.) The emphasis of this program is on training teachers to understand bullying and intervene appropriately.

Prevention and a schoolwide culture that fosters positive approaches to problem solving are key features. One excellent aspect of this program is that it directly addresses teacher beliefs and common myths that foster bullying behavior. Some of the teacher beliefs that the authors claim maintain bullying include "Bullying is child's play," "Only male children bully," and "I won't see bullying because it happens to and from school and not during the school day" (Horne, Orpinas, Newman-Carlson, and Bartolomucci, 2004, p. 315).

Some common myths that the authors say teachers believe about bullying are that it is a "normal part of childhood," that children will outgrow it, and that intervening makes it worse (Horne, Orpinas, Newman-Carlson, and Bartolomucci, 2004, p. 309). The following is an example of how teacher attitudes and behaviors can inadvertently foster an atmosphere conducive to bullying by favoring one social group or type of student over another.

Reality Check

Josef is an intellectually gifted student in Mr. Pena's fourth grade class. Josef is verbal, opinionated, well read, and a poor athlete. He is frequently teased by students when he answers questions in class or performs poorly in a game, both of which he frequently does. Over time, Josef has become verbally hostile to the other students, calling them stupid and laughing when they make academic errors. Their bullying behavior has escalated and now includes tripping and pushing of Josef in the halls.

Mr. Pena has told Josef that he will have to change or no one will like him. Mr. Pena admitted to the school mental health professional that he has not stepped in to stop the teasing because he can understand why the other students do not like Josef. He thinks Josef needs to learn that others don't like him.

Teachers (like all of us) sometimes fail to realize the unintended impact of their actions. A male fourth grade teacher has a great deal of influence on the behavior of his students, especially his male students. Even if Mr. Pena does not openly admit or even feel a dislike for Josef, by allowing others to tease him without penalty, he shows a preference for them. He is modeling an understanding of them and their opinions, but not of Josef and his.

What should Mr. Pena do? He should make it clear that teasing is unacceptable in his classroom. He should demonstrate that he values Josef's intellectual ability as much as he values the athletic capability of the others. He should deliver negative consequences to Josef when he makes fun of the others for their errors and to the others when they pick on Josef. Mr. Pena should also carefully scrutinize his own behavior to be sure that he is not contributing to Josef's reputation by, for example, looking annoyed when he volunteers to answer yet another question.

A useful technique for enhancing reputations of students who are not well liked is to give them a leadership position in the class, but then provide careful guidance on how it is carried out. For example, Mr. Pena might give Josef the opportunity to lead a study group, but school him carefully on the importance of complimenting his fellow students on their work, assisting them when they have difficulty, and giving them a chance to contribute. Mr. Pena should voice his belief to the entire class that Josef will do a good job and then compliment Josef publicly on a job well done. The crucial issue here is the teacher's guidance to be sure Josef does perform his duties well.

Teachers who would like to see schoolwide antibullying programs adopted in their schools might begin with reading "Best Practices in Bullying Prevention" (a chapter in *Best Practices in School Psychology V*), a review of bullying research and antibullying programs by Felix and Furlong (2008). Two excellent books covering all aspects of the bullying problem are *Bullying in American Schools*, by Espelage and Swearer (2004), and *Bullying Prevention and Intervention: Realistic Strategies for Schools*, by Swearer, Espelage, and Napolitano (2009).

Cyberbullying

Cyberbullying is the use of electronic methods to intimidate, isolate, or harm relationships of the victim. It may be perpetrated by one individual or a group on another individual or group. The effect of this form of bullying is far reaching due to the large numbers of people who can receive these messages in short periods of time, the fact that the harmful material has staying power, and the reality that the perpetrators may be unknown. It also presents some unique challenges to schools because, although students can be greatly affected at school, the act itself may take place away from school grounds.

The most important thing for teachers to keep in mind is that cyberbullying is bullying, and it is harmful. In two cases that received high levels of media attention, 15-year-old Phoebe Prince and 13-year-old Megan Meier both committed suicide following incidents of extreme attacks online. Cyberbullying can be dangerous.

As in identifying other forms of bullying, teachers will find it helpful to be aware of which students are isolated from the others or show difficulty in social interaction. They should also be aware of which students are leaders but use that trait to lead others astray. More specifically, teachers should do the following:

- monitor the use of computers and other electronic devices in their classroom
- make it clear to students that no behavior should take place online that would be wrong if it were done in person
- make it understood to students that their inappropriate electronic behavior can be traced back to them
- keep communication open with students regarding their online activity
- advocate for schoolwide technology education programs for parents
- encourage schoolwide assessment of the degree of cyberbullying taking place
- support the inclusion of cyberbullying in the school's antibullying program
- be aware of the laws related to the use of technology and electronic social sites in their state

Relational Aggression

Relational aggression is a form of bullying in which perpetrators use their relationship with the victim and/or with others to intimidate, isolate, and harm the victim. The following comments illustrate the circumstances of relational aggression:

- I won't play with you if you play with her.
- I won't go to your party if you ask her.
- Let's all have a secret password. If we don't tell them, they won't be able to play with us.
- If we tell him she had sex with his friend, he will be sure to never date her again.

Relational aggression can take place in any age group. There is some evidence that it is more prevalent among girls than boys, although boys are not immune. In adolescence, when relationships and social groups involve boys and girls, both may be involved.

The concept of relational aggression is more difficult for educators to grasp than that of other bullying forms. After all, no student should be expected to invite everyone to her party or be friends with everyone equally. Should the teacher really get involved in student social relationships to this degree? The following are some things that the teacher can consider to determine whether what is taking place is really relational aggression or simply social preference:

- Students have the right to choose their own friends, but not the friends of others. Using a relationship to prevent someone else from having friends is aggression.
- Spreading rumors about someone with the intent of limiting their friendships is aggression.
- Using your talent for leadership to prevent someone else from having friends, getting a date, or having a positive reputation is aggression.
- Taking advantage of an imbalance of social power by targeting someone who is already isolated or intimidated is aggression.

Relational aggression harms school climate and leads to negative effects on the part of victims who, as in other forms of bullying, are more likely to be truant and less likely to do their best academically. Education about relational aggression is a good place for schools to start in combating this problem. Younger children, especially, may just be trying to make and keep friends and may not see their behavior as a form of bullying. Education helps to sensitize them to the issue.

Teachers should group students differently on different occasions and not allow them to self-select. This avoids anyone being left out by the group and also gives students the opportunity to work with several people in the class, not just their friends. Teachers should also be active participants in student interaction. If only one student is left out of a party invitation, for example, teachers should consider getting the advice of the school counselor on how to address the issue or contact the parent involved in setting up the party.

Finally, teachers should remember that social isolation is a risk factor and should be addressed even if it seems understandable due to a student's very different characteristics or lack of social skills. The creation of an environment that is welcoming to different types of students is the educator's responsibility.

Gender Identity and Bullying

Until relatively recently, gender identity was not a focus of the bullying literature. Perhaps bullying with regard to gender identity is more prevalent now because the issue is getting more attention in the general culture, and especially in the media. Perhaps it has always played a role, and most mental health professionals did not tend to it before. The shooting death of Lawrence King (see chapter 1) certainly brought media focus on the issue.

In a 2008 study of boys in ninth to eleventh grades attending an all-male private school, 48% said they had been bullied, and 26% of those said they had been called gay (Swearer, Turner, Givens, and Pollack, 2008). Of all of those bullied, those who were called gay suffered the most psychological impact. There is also evidence in other research that characteristics and behaviors associated with being gay may enhance the likelihood of being targeted by bullies.

The main point here for teachers is that name calling, making fun, and teasing related to gender identity is bullying regardless of whether the target is gay, lesbian, bisexual, transgender, or not. It still creates a negative environment for those who are targeted, as well as for the rest of the school community. Issues related to sexual identity should be part of the school's antibullying program and should be treated as any other form of bullying or name calling. It is aggression.

THOUGHT PROCESSES OF
AGGRESSIVE/HOSTILE STUDENTS

Students who eventually act out in an aggressive manner have often adopted a way of thinking or reacting to things that occur in their world that leads them to aggression. Teachers of young children can have an influence on that thinking by helping their students explain events in positive or at least neutral terms and helping them evaluate alternative behavioral reactions.

For example, Fred and Carl are both in second grade. Going down the hall to their remedial reading class, Fred calls Carl a pig. Carl pushes Fred against the wall. Instead of just sending Carl to the office, the teacher might ask Carl what he was thinking and what other things he could have done in reaction to those thoughts that might have been more effective, or, at least, would not have gotten him in more trouble than Fred. Alternatives might be to tell the teacher, tell Carl to stop, tell Carl what he thinks of him, and so forth. (Teachers interested in learning more about helping students make effective behavioral choices should also see Palmatier's *Crisis Counseling for a Quality School Community* [1998]). Fred, on the other hand, might learn from Carl, with the teacher's help, what it feels like to be insulted. The teacher can also tell Fred what she thinks and how it makes her feel when she hears one of her students insulting someone.

We speak of "teachable moments" in academics. If we took more advantage of these moments for teaching appropriate behavior to young children, we might decrease the incidence of aggression in older students. Some teachers respond to the previously mentioned suggestions by saying, "I do that"; however, when one observes what they do, one hears the teacher saying something like, to Fred, "Just because he called you a name doesn't mean you have the right to push him." Or, to Carl, "How would you like it if he called you a pig? The next time you call anybody a name, I am going to let them call you one. Then you will see what it feels like." This is no more than a monologue by the teacher. All that is being experienced by the children is that they are in trouble. To learn anything from the incident, students must generate and evaluate the alternative behaviors themselves. If there is not time to deal with the incident when it happens, later is better than letting it go altogether.

A WORD ABOUT ZERO TOLERANCE

In several of the aforementioned instances, it has been suggested that teachers be clear regarding the unacceptability of aggressive, hostile, or abusive behavior. This is, indeed, an important message; however, there is ample research that suggests that simply removing offending students from school does little to change their future behavior and may actually make it worse. And, of course, they eventually come back to school. Even in the rare instances when they do not return to the place of learning, they are still in the community. While appropriate consequences can be an important part of a program leading to behavior change, instruction, guidance, and involvement of support systems at home and at school are essential.

SUMMARY

In this chapter, we discussed the signs and signals of which teachers should be aware to avoid escalation in interaction with hostile or aggressive students. Teachers were advised to hold steady and communicate clearly. The importance of an audience, teaching moments, and a problem-solving orientation were discussed. Various forms of bullying and antibullying programs were described.

CHAPTER 8

Parents in Crisis

Family support requires collaboration and coordination between home and school, and all the issues that affect this relationship must be addressed.

—Bowman, 1994, p. 68

Many of the events that precipitate crises in students will affect or originate in the family. Steele and Raider (1991), in their book *Working with Families in Crisis: School-Based Intervention*, list six forms of family crisis. See table 8.1 for descriptions and examples.

Not all crisis events evolve from what would normally be considered negative experiences. A wedding or birth of a sibling, a family move due to a parent's promotion, or the remarriage of a parent can all create tension in a family and necessitate reordering and a change in roles. Teachers should be aware of the potential impact of even these more positive occurrences on the behavior and emotions of their students.

Teachers will often become involved in one of two more intense family crises. The first is the one in which the teacher's student has been traumatized. Examples of this form of family crisis are when a child is sexually abused, sees a family member killed, or is involved in an accident. The second form is one in which the parents are in crisis and are concerned about the impact on the child. Examples of this form are parental divorce or an extramarital affair, terminal illness in a parent, or family violence.

Table 8.1. Forms of Family Crisis

Extrafamilial	war, natural disaster	crises that happen outside the family
Intrafamilial	divorce, abuse	crises that happen inside the family
Dismemberment	death of member, member leaves home	loss of family member
Ascension	birth, grandmother moves in	addition of family member
Demoralization	substance abuse, extramarital affair	unwanted behavior of a family member
Demoralization with Dismemberment or Ascension	suicide, psychiatric hospitalization, teen pregnancy	member loss associated with unwanted behavior or member addition associated with unwanted behavior

Source: Steele, W., and M. Raider. (1991). *Working with Families in Crisis: School-Based Intervention*. New York: Guilford. Reprinted with permission.

FAMILIES OF THE TRAUMATIZED CHILD

When a child experiences some form of trauma, parents often come to the teacher to explain the situation and get advice. Especially in low-income communities, the teacher may be the only child-related professional the parents know or to whom they have easy access. Pediatricians may not be the same from one clinic visit to the next, and there may be a stigma or bias against consulting mental health professionals; therefore, it is important that teachers be knowledgeable about student reaction to trauma.

Often, knowing that the teacher is watchful and concerned will relieve some of the parents' anxiety. Teachers can provide information to parents on what behaviors to expect from the child. They can keep parents informed regarding the child's interaction with peers at school and his or her academic performance, both of which are important indicators of psychological adjustment. Information provided by the teacher to a community or school mental health professional can be important in the formulation of treatment plans for a student.

Teachers should not underestimate the value of their contribution to both families and clinicians working with traumatized children. Their frame of reference due to extensive experience with children and knowledge of the child in question, both before and after the event, are invaluable. Teachers also provide consistency of routine for children in crisis and diversionary activities that can take the child's mind away from negative experiences. Success in school is a great antidote for unpleasantness elsewhere in a student's life.

Teachers can also normalize parental reactions. The concept of normalization is an important one in crisis intervention. Normalization is communication to parents that their reactions are to be expected given their situation.

Reality Check

The Cochran family has just found out that their 10-year-old daughter, Juanita, has been sexually abused by her uncle. Child protective services are involved, and Juanita is in therapy. Mrs. Cochran has informed Mrs. King, Juanita's teacher, because she wants Mrs. King to let her know if Juanita shows any effects of the experience while she is in school.

Mrs. Cochran called Mrs. King every afternoon for the first week after she found out about the abuse. She apologized profusely for calling so often but explained that she was really worried about Juanita. Mrs. King normalized Mrs. Cochran's concern by saying that any mother would worry under the circumstances, and she willingly spoke with Mrs. Cochran each time she called. During the second week, Mrs. Cochran called only once. By the end of the first month, Mrs. Cochran was comfortable with having Mrs. King call her if she saw anything in Juanita's behavior that was cause for concern.

In this example, Mrs. King was supportive, understanding, and patient. Had Mrs. King been unwilling to talk to Mrs. Cochran, or if Mrs. King had told Mrs. Cochran that she was calling too often, Mrs. King would have cut off a source of support to Mrs. Cochran. Mrs. King would also have increased the mother's anxiety about her child and perhaps her own psychological state. What Mrs. King did may not have been therapy, but it was therapeutic.

PARENTS WHO HAVE EXPERIENCED TRAUMA

Teachers can make similar contributions when the parents are the ones who have experienced the trauma. Parents may be more reluctant to discuss their own difficulties than they would be to talk about those of their child. Since children stand to benefit a great deal from supportive environments at school when things at home are stressful, teachers should work toward a relationship with parents that will make them willing to share concerns with the teacher.

Which teacher behaviors help to create such an impression? For the most part, they are the same as those that foster positive and open communication in any relationship: patience, a positive attitude, and a willingness to communicate. Specific behaviors that a teacher can employ to foster positive relationships with parents are as follows:

- initiating periodic communication with parents
- communicating an awareness of a student's strengths and not just his or her weaknesses
- taking time to talk to parents who initiate communication
- being willing to alter classroom or homework requirements when there is a special student or family need
- fostering positive communication between parents of students in the class and other school personnel, for example, the school nurse or principal
- demonstrating a willingness to listen to parental concerns or criticisms without becoming defensive

Teachers who engage in these behaviors give the message that they welcome parents as partners, and they are more likely to be informed when parents are experiencing a crisis. How should teachers react when parents reveal information about a family crisis? Many of the listening skills previously discussed apply here. Take time to listen, and avoid attempts to solve the problem or give advice. Listen carefully for what the parent is asking from you. Does she want you to monitor the school behavior of the child and let her know how the child is doing? Or, are you perhaps being asked if you have noticed anything that is of concern?

Maybe the parent is asking for a referral for the child to an appropriate mental health professional and does not know where to begin. Maybe the parent is reaching out to find help for herself. The request may not be stated. You may have to interpret what they are asking based on what is being said. You should always check with the parent by asking how you might be of help and offering some different ways you think you might be of assistance. Remember that the family's personal information is being revealed to you as a professional and not as a friend; therefore, you must focus on your professional area of expertise—children and their education.

If parents ask if you have noticed anything different in the student's behavior, it is certainly within your area of expertise to give an opinion. If they ask if the child gets along with other children in the classroom or if his or her peer relations have changed, you can also offer your opinion in that area. You can comment on anything that relates to your experience with children under similar circumstances to those presented, assuming that you have the experience.

You are also likely to know whether changes in school workload are advisable and how they might be made. You will know whether the quality of the child's academic work has changed. In short, you know a lot about what concerns parents with regard to their children. You also know how to access school mental health services for students and their families. You are a valuable resource to families in crisis.

BEING SUPPORTIVE, PROFESSIONAL, AND TRUTHFUL

Parent-teacher conferences are a common form of home-school communication at most schools. Face-to-face meetings help the teacher learn more about what parents in crisis need. They also serve to clarify the plan for helping the student and the roles of the adults in carrying out the plan. These conferences sometimes lack focus and are full of generalities that do not lead to concrete action. Specificity and clarity are important in coping with a crisis event. Chapter 10 provides more information about effective parent-teacher conferences. Here we will note some guidelines for enhancing communication at parent-teacher conferences under stressful circumstances.

At the end of your meetings with parents (or phone calls if meetings cannot be arranged), always summarize what you and the parent agreed each would do. Be sure to set up a form of communication for the future and a time frame for the contact. End the meeting with a positive but honest comment about the child and the parent's contact with you. Honest is a key word here. Sometimes positive comments that are not true can do more harm than good. Do not say that you are sure the child will come through the experience just fine. You have no way of knowing that. Do not say that the child is doing well academically if that is not so. Parents will want to know why you said that and then gave the child a D on his report. Remember, professional interactions are characterized by forthright professional opinions based on solid information. You may tell your friend you like her dress if you don't. You should not tell a parent a child is doing well when he or she is not.

Timing and formulation of comments are part of your professional responsibility. When the family is in crisis may not be the time to talk about academic issues, unless they are quite significant, and the child's positive characteristics should always be part of the conversation, along with his needs.

There are some pitfalls that the teacher should try to avoid in aiding families in crisis. One is that, in an effort to be helpful, we may talk about things we do not understand all that well. For example, should a student who is on medication for attention deficit/hyperactivity disorder take more or less medication when the family is in crisis? That is not a question a teacher is equipped to answer; however, it would be appropriate to advise the parent to check with the child's physician.

Another potential problem is that we may give advice based on what has worked for us or on our personal beliefs without evidence that it would be helpful to others. Telling a parent to go to church, smooth things over with an estranged spouse, or get a job is advice giving not based on the teacher's area of expertise and is inappropriate professional behavior.

FAMILIES OF DIFFERENT CULTURES

Teachers sometimes feel inadequate to the task of assisting families from cultural groups other than their own. The sense that these groups are different and that you cannot help if you don't know the culture can lead to reluctance to engage these families. This is unfortunate, because often it is these families who lack access to professional supports outside of the school. They are also likely to know less about how to navigate the American system to get the help they need.

Certainly, it is advisable to learn as much as possible about the populations with which you work, especially if there is one large, prevalent group represented. However, a student's family needs may arise before the teacher has achieved a high level of cultural expertise, or there may be so many cultural groups represented at the school that awareness of all of them is not possible. There are several ways teachers can be helpful to multicultural families in crisis, even without extensive knowledge of their cultures. To prepare to meet the needs of multicultural families in crisis, teachers should do the following:

- Research the culture to learn more.
- Become acquainted with school personnel from the culture in question, if possible, to obtain a realistic and informal understanding of the group.
- Obtain tips for best practices in using interpreters in schools through reading and consultation with support personnel.
- Become aware of the group's behavior with regard to life events most likely to be related to crises, such as death rituals, reactions to individuals with disabilities, the role of and expectations for children when the family is under stress, and the willingness to access mental health services.

We will talk more about multicultural families when we address prevention in the next section.

MILITARY FAMILIES

Approximately 1.5 million students in U.S. public schools have at least one parent in the military (Military Child Initiative Home Page, 2010). Research on the impact of a military connection on the development of children is mixed. Some shows positive effects, including maturity, flexibility, and advanced social skills. Other studies suggest academic and emotional difficulties associated with frequent moves and parental absences, although not a lot is known about the impact on children of parent deployment during war.

A recent study of school adjustment of military adolescents is especially interesting, because students and parents, as well as school staff, were interviewed (Bradshaw, Sudhinaraset, Mmari, and Blum, 2010). Of most concern to military parents were difficulties in making transitions from school to school, for example, schools requiring new testing each time a child with special needs was registered, and missed instruction due to different curricula from school to school.

Students were most concerned with difficulties in making friends and participating in extracurricular activities. Some students felt that only other military students could really understand their situation and that support staff, such as guidance counselors, were uninformed regarding their needs.

Research with students from military families is consistent with educational research in general. Connection with school is of major importance in student academic and social/emotional development, and that connection is made, in large part, through positive contact with adults in the environment. Again, teachers make a difference. In addition to showing interest and getting to know the students, the Military Child Initiative website suggests that schools work to do the following:

- Partner new students with current students for welcoming and orientation.
- Be flexible in allowing students who are late registrants to enter the classes they need.
- Be flexible in allowing student athletes to be part of teams through such mechanisms as prior coach documentation of ability, video tryouts, and holding spaces open for latecomers.
- Develop academic plans for students that can follow them from school to school to avoid duplication and missed instruction.
- Utilize electronic means to help students catch up on missed instruction without having to retake entire courses.

Since our of knowledge of how schools should address the needs of students whose parents are deployed during war is limited, suggestions on how to assist any one student whose parent is deployed must be made with caution. Some advise allowing military students to share experiences with the class or having the class follow war-related occurrences, but use caution here. We can't assume that all students would appreciate the attention or focus on their situation. As in other areas, it is best to know the student, talk to the parent, and then decide.

SUMMARY

In this chapter, we discussed the unique position teachers are in to assist parents in crisis. Whether the child has been traumatized or the crisis focuses on the parents, the teacher can help by listening, providing valuable information on the child's behavior in school, and helping parents navigate systems that can offer support. Teachers should make an effort to learn about the impact various cultural beliefs and behaviors may have on the family's reaction to crisis, but they should not hesitate to assist just because they are not experts in the family's cultural traditions. Those in areas where military families reside should make a special effort to attend to their needs for belonging and flexibility.

MORE THAN AN OUNCE OF PREVENTION

CHAPTER 9

Being Prepared and Setting a Positive Tone

In addition to improved academic functioning, supportive student-teacher relationships are linked to positive peer relations and decreases in suicidal ideations, externalizing behaviors, emotional distress, violence, substance abuse and sexual activity.

—Suldo et al., 2009, p. 69

PLANNING

The Classroom Environment

There is ample evidence to support a connection between environment and human reactions. Environments perceived as unfriendly lead to fear and anxiety reactions in their inhabitants. The concurrent physiological responses reduce ability to reason, increase the likelihood of habitual or impulsive responses, and have the potential to increase physical strength. These are the things of which a full-blown crisis is made.

I once visited a classroom where small plants in plastic pots decorated the tables, and several reading chairs with lamps were in the corners of the room. The message to the students was clear: This is your space, and you may have a need for one place or another in the room during a day. This room represented a break from the institutional routine, and its tone showed respect for the students as individuals. The atmosphere was relaxing. Its very look made one want to be quiet and concentrate on the task at hand.

Environment can have a preventative impact in other ways. Advance planning is an important factor in crisis avoidance. While most teachers know how to set up a classroom for maximum effectiveness with regard to learning, few consider the importance of the classroom plan for crisis prevention. Students should have sufficient space between them to avoid negative interactions. Teachers should move around the room to enhance their presence and student contact.

When the teacher is at his desk, that desk should be a place from which the whole classroom can be seen. The desk location should also give the teacher a line of vision into the hall if the classroom door is left open. The desk should be clear of heavy objects or anything that could be used as a weapon, for example, scissors or a letter opener. Even books, which are obviously important furnishings in classrooms, should be housed on shelves and not on the teacher's desk, the area where an emotional encounter with a student is most likely to occur. Bricks and stones, sometimes used as doorstops in older schools, should be avoided, as should heavy bookends.

Above all else, the school's crisis response plan should be accessible and in a format that is easy to read under pressure. If your district does not provide an abbreviated form of the crisis plan that is tabbed and easy to access, make one yourself and keep it readily available. Be sure to update your abbreviated plan if the larger school plan is changed.

The Classroom Routine

Appropriate, well-known routines and procedures are not only helpful in managing student behavior, but they can actually be comforting to students under stress when other areas of life may be unpredictable. Advance planning and organization also help the teacher concentrate less on getting the daily activities right and more on student needs; therefore, visible classroom rules, a written schedule for the day, and preparation for any change in routine should be part of every teacher's way of doing business.

Classroom rules should be written positively. "We listen while others are speaking," for example, is better than, "Don't talk when someone else is talking." Rules should be discussed at the beginning of the school year and periodically thereafter to ensure student understanding.

Students whose schedules differ from the class, such as those who go to a resource room, should have separate schedules taped to their desks or on the wall near their desks. Dependable routines that can be easily reviewed reduce anxiety. If a student cannot read, small pictures representing the day's activities can be used.

We all have days when we are not at our best. If we are lucky, we have the luxury of changing our plans for those days and going a little easier on ourselves. Students in school rarely have that opportunity. Their days are planned for them, and their schedules are often full. If one adds to this lack of flexibility the frustration that some students face because of academic failure, bullying, or lack of social success, one sees how the potential for disruptive behavior can grow.

A wise teacher will note signs of frustration or a day that is just going sour for a student and allow flexibility in routine. Perhaps the homework assignment can be turned in one day late, or the test missed when the student was ill can be put off a day. Maybe the student can stay in and read a book instead of going out to recess. Above all, the teacher should avoid adding to the student's frustration by commenting on less than important infractions or breaches of routine. This flexibility leads to a better emotional tone in class and more trusting and open relationships with students. There is a difference between disorganization and flexibility.

Students should be given the opportunity for quiet time during the day and some time alone to read in a corner or work on a puzzle. Many students eligible for special education will spend several minutes in a day going from one room to another or will miss instruction in their main classroom while they are in a resource room. When they return they are behind and sometimes lost. They need time to get settled and assistance in catching up. Teachers may not always have a say in scheduling, but they can alter their class requirements or plans to help relieve the stress on these students.

School lunchrooms can be centers of nearly complete chaos if student numbers are large and schedules are less than perfectly aligned. Consider giving students a brief time after lunch or recess to relax quietly before moving on to the next activity. This down time also allows students to cool off after playground encounters that may have been stressful.

One of the most important preventative classroom techniques is good teaching. Students presented with material at their instructional level are much more likely to stay focused than those who are given work at their frustration level (too difficult) or at their mastery level (too easy). Knowing the instructional level of your students is essential for good classroom management. A variety of teaching techniques and appropriate pacing are also important. Too many worksheets and not enough active learning, for example, can contribute to behavior problems in the classroom.

Discipline

Most schools have a discipline policy and, while teachers may have been represented on the committee that developed the policy, the procedures are rarely influenced by any one teacher. However, the route by which students get involved with the school's disciplinary process is usually through the classroom teacher; therefore, teachers have a great deal of impact on who gets disciplined, if not how.

If your school frequently utilizes zero tolerance, suspension, and other forms of punishment, the last opportunity a student has to change behavior through a more positive influence may rest with you. Every teacher should have behavior management procedures that are known to the class. The procedures should include expectations and reinforcement for meeting them. They should apply to all students. Consequences for not meeting the requirements, however, may need to be different for different situations.

Students should know that they are expected to meet class requirements. If they do not, they will be asked to see the teacher so a plan for meeting the expectations can be worked out. The message here is two-fold, first that the requirements must be met, and second, that students will be given assistance in finding a way to meet them if they are having trouble.

Teachers should have a number of "tricks" in their bags for helping students meet expectations, whether they are of a behavioral or academic type. Whenever possible, students should be involved in deciding what method will be tried. Least intrusive methods should be utilized first. For example, if a third grader is not turning in homework, the teacher might find out if the child is writing down the assignment, bringing the right books home, or trying the assignment and finding it too difficult. The first intervention should be related to the most obvious problem. If the student is not writing down the assignment, a notebook might be provided that he can cover with his favorite stickers.

The teacher should start with a verbal reminder the first week; then move to a nonverbal signal; and then finally give the child a week to copy assignments on his own, being sure to comment on his success. Having the student record and then graph his own improvement in doing assignments can serve as a reward for the behavior and teaches him a way to monitor his own performance.

Compare the effect of this approach on classroom climate to one where all students who do not complete assignments get a note sent home or go to the principal's office after missing three assignments. These consequences are negative, take the control away from the student and the teacher, and do not model a problem-solving approach for children.

In a book describing best practices for school psychologists, Bear, Cavalier, and Manning (2002) note that, "A teacher's punishment-oriented style toward discipline not only fails to promote social-emotional competencies and prosocial behavior in the student, but also provides negative models of behavior, thereby further impeding the student's social and emotional development" (p. 979). These specialists admit that negative consequences are sometimes necessary; however, they recommend that consequences always be accompanied by instruction on how to improve the behavior.

Teachers should consult with mental health/educational specialist service providers in the school before behavior or academic problems become severe. Waiting until the behavior is habitual, dangerous, or even just a significant frustration makes it harder for the intervention to be successful.

Dress

Most teachers must dress comfortably to get through a day that requires many hours on their feet, walking to widely separated parts of the school building, carrying books and papers, and maintaining their classrooms; however, teacher dress serves other functions in schools. It gives messages to students and parents that can, in small ways, contribute to crisis prevention. And, it can foster or hinder performance during a crisis.

Professional dress suggests that one is in control and, if the teacher is young, helps maintain a degree of distance from the student's age group that can help in managing misbehavior. This is especially important at the secondary level. Teachers who wear short skirts, dye their hair in colors popular with the students, or wear flip-flops to class are inviting challenges from students who may be too likely to see them as peers rather than authority figures. For older teachers, the problem may be a perception of so much distance from the students that there is trouble making meaningful contact. For them, dropping the suit and tie may be helpful, especially if they are new to the school and do not have the advantage of being known personally.

The issue of dress is also relevant to relationships with parents. Here first impressions are important because parents usually spend limited amounts of time with their child's teacher. A good guideline for beginning teachers is to ask themselves, "What type of dress is likely to inspire confidence in parents who have little to go on but first impressions?" Would seeing a teacher in spiked heels lead a parent to feel that the teacher is practical and child oriented?

It is important to consider mainstream values and impressions here, not what can be proven. For example, I have no idea if tattooed teachers are better or worse in the classroom than those who are not tattooed; however, I think it would be fair to say that most parents would be more likely to question the seriousness and reliability of a teacher covered with tattoos. This is not about fashion or money spent but an overall professional image.

Teachers who work with aggressive or acting out students have other issues to consider with regard to dress. Long hair, earrings, scarves, and ties invite pulling. Shoes with high heels impede movement, as do very long or tight skirts. Teachers in any setting can face circumstances that might require leaving the building quickly. A spare sweater or jacket and hat left in the classroom closet, as well as a pair of walking shoes that can get wet, are likely to be beneficial.

It is also important to consider what will have to be taken along if the class must leave the building. Usually this will be, at a minimum, the class roster with parents' addresses and phone numbers and the teacher's personal things, like wallet, purse, keys, and medications. So, it is a good idea to have a tote available.

Many school crisis teams (see chapter 11) will provide teachers with sun screen, bug spray, first aid kits, and other materials that should leave the building with the class. If your school does not provide these items, consider obtaining them for yourself but bringing the need to the attention of the school administration as soon as possible.

AWARENESS

How often have we said, "If only I had known." Wouldn't we all like to be that gentleman in the television series who knew everything the day before it appeared in the newspaper? It is not likely we will ever know the future; however, with the proper training and confidence in our intuition, many of us could improve our level of foresight. Foresight is enhanced by communication, sensitivity, knowledge of which signs are important, and a willingness to have confidence in our impressions and take action.

A simple daily exercise can enhance our awareness and lead to better communication. At the end of each day, the teacher should consider the students he or she encountered during that day and ask the question, "Did everyone seem okay?" That simple question disciplines us to reflect on our impressions. Without censoring your thoughts, let your mind flow. You will usually think of things like, Susy had a cold, Larry got angry at Sam, and Kisha giggled through the video. Maybe there was something more to note, like the new student who spoke to a peer for the first time, or Maria is getting teased. These are mental notes worth making. When patterns are noticed, it is time to use your communication skills to explore causes.

Communication in this context is not intended to mean probing questions about a student's private life. Observing, writing notes on student papers, inviting parents to a conference, offering to help a student after school, and even a smile as a student enters your room are all forms of communication that say, "I am willing to listen, if you want to talk." Keen observation and listening skills are the key pieces to awareness.

What to Look For

What does a teacher look for to determine which students are at risk? How does she avoid crying wolf? No list of risk signals is foolproof, and, of course, trouble can occur with none of the expected signs present. The following list suggests some characteristics that warrant further assessment. Remember, a teacher does not have to be convinced that a crisis is coming to further evaluate a situation or refer a student for support service. The risk is not in addressing a situation that turns out to be benign, but in failing to address one that is serious. Please note that the intention here is not to discipline the student, but to avail the student of support services that could be helpful. Mental health professionals in the schools can then take the responsibility to determine whether in-depth service should be provided. The following are student behaviors that can warrant investigation:

- appearing to be lost or in a daze
- difficulty concentrating
- excessive self-blame
- irritability and/or emotional outbursts
- mood swings
- appearing sad
- diminished interest in activities
- restlessness
- failing to complete work when an attempt has been made
- social isolation
- excessive weight loss or gain
- poor grooming

Debunking the Myths

An important part of awareness is being able to separate fact from fiction regarding behavior and risk factors among students. While often teachers know at a cognitive level that child abuse can take place in all socioeconomic and ethnic groups, for example, many will still be less likely to recognize signs in families they consider to be mainstream. There is evidence that sociable, popular students can still be bullies (Farmer, 2000), yet how many teachers are likely to pick up on that behavior among students who are well-liked and even leaders? Another example is that many teachers are more likely to expect social and emotional problems among students identified as intellectually gifted, when, in fact, research suggests that group is quite well adjusted (Gust-Brey and Cross, 1999; Lehman and Erdwins, 2004). Are we more likely to expect trouble from the student with blue hair than the cheerleader? Is that assumption based on facts?

Newsweek printed the following quote from the principal in Paducah, Kentucky, where 14-year-old Michael Carneal killed three of his classmates:

> His father's a deacon, and his sister's the valedictorian. Michael never dressed in black or wore upside-down crosses. He does not fit the mold of what our society says an angry person should be like. (Pedersen and Van Boven, 1997, p. 30)

The article went on to describe the Carneals as a "model family." The important issue here is to examine our biases. Most of us assume that we may be subject to ethnic bias. Fewer are willing to explore their biases with regard to economic status, appearance, what makes a "good" as opposed to a "problem child," and appropriate ways to express emotion.

VISIBILITY

For the elementary teacher, awareness also means physical presence. Rather than sitting at your desk after you give an assignment, walk around the room to see who understands it and who does not. Rather than standing in one spot on the playground or while on bus duty, walk around, listen to what is said, and observe situations to which your knowledge and intuition have alerted you.

When with groups of children, focus on them and not on your fellow teachers. Visit the school lunchroom, even if aides have lunch duty. As most teachers know, lunch and recess tell us a lot about the relationships among children.

If you are a secondary teacher, physical presence is harder to attain due to the size of the school and number of students you see in a day; however, teachers who spend time in the halls and stairways, watch who goes to lunch alone, know the types of groups students belong to, and see who has a problem in handling common social situations will be well ahead in foreseeing which students will have difficulties.

Teachers or aides who congregate together when they might be among the students decrease their own potential for awareness of student behaviors and suggest a lack of interest in students. As many adults as possible should be visible before and after school, during extracurricular activities, and between classes.

Visibility combined with a failure to respond to student infractions communicates the wrong message. Teachers say, for example, that they intervene in student harassment and bullying. Studies of student reports generally show that students do not believe teachers intervene, at least not often enough (Holt and Keyes, 2004). Adults must be not just physically present but also involved. Visibility not only creates an atmosphere of control and organization for students, but it can give the same message to intruders in playgrounds and school halls. Again, however, adults who notice a stranger and assume that someone else will question him or her do not enhance safety in schools.

LISTENING

What if the student does want to talk? It may sound overly obvious to say that the teacher should listen; however, in the busy life of a teacher, this is not always easy. Because children and adolescents are more spontaneous than most adults, they may not choose the most appropriate moment to reveal themselves to the teacher. Nevertheless, they may have chosen a given moment due to the pressure for relief from a thought or feeling, and that could give the moment added importance and potential for crisis prevention.

When possible, the teacher should take advantage of any moment for communication presented by the student, within reason. This is especially important for the reticent student; however, there are also students who have a regular need to talk. To permit them to choose the time and place is unrealistic and can lead to further adjustment difficulties. For these students, routine times, set and limited by the teacher, might be appropriate. These brief but regular meetings should soon be sufficient to reveal the degree of student need and whether referral for support service is necessary.

What is listening? Unfortunately, when interacting with children, what many adults call listening is really talking, taking the opportunity to tell the child something that we think he or she should know. Busy teachers may be especially vulnerable to this behavior because of the limited time they have to spend with each student and the many things children and adolescents seem to need to be told. As difficult as it may be, this temptation must be avoided in favor of open-ended questions and nonjudgmental responses, at least until the nature of the problem or circumstance is fully grasped.

This suggests another landmine in our adult-child communication, which is the tendency to believe we "get the picture" long before it is truly revealed. True communication takes time. When the time is not available at the moment, another time should be rescheduled to pick up the conversation. With younger children, the teacher should be prepared to help the child recall the nature of the prior discussion. The fact that the child may not remember later does not necessarily lessen the importance of exploring the topic.

Two questions that teachers often ask regarding personal conversations with students are To what degree should I tell the student how to fix the problem?, and Should I promise to keep the communication confidential? Unless the student is in immediate danger or is a threat to others, it is almost always more important to keep the line of communication open than it is to solve the problem.

Indeed, the mistake we often make as adults communicating with youth is to offer simple solutions to the presenting problem. A more helpful response is to model important skills in problem solving. Some of the skills suggested by Carroll (1997) are clarifying the problem, giving information, listing choices, and providing encouragement.

It is not uncommon, especially for teens, to request confidentiality before revealing a concern. Legal factors, as well as best practice in crisis prevention, leave the teacher with few options in this regard. Confidentiality cannot be promised as a condition of communication between teacher and student. In most cases, honesty regarding this issue, if handled carefully, will lead to more respect from the student for the adult, not less.

Whether or not this is the case, students must be told that the teacher, as a responsible adult with the youth's best interest in mind, will take whatever measures are necessary to protect the student or other students involved. It should also be made clear that this does not mean that a teacher will pass along sensitive information to other students or teachers, if their safety is not a factor.

A common occurrence in many classrooms is the discouragement of "tattling" or reporting the misbehavior of other students to the teacher. This behavior can be annoying, and some teachers probably discourage it because it also hurts the reputation of the teller and disrupts the class; however, we must consider the long-range impact of teaching students not to seek the assistance of the adults in charge and not to report the rule breaking they see. Indeed, one might argue that Columbine and Jonesboro are examples of failure to tattle taken to its extreme.

The best approach for the teacher here is to consider every report from a student on its merits and not to have a class rule against "tattling." If a child repeatedly tells you about minor infractions of other students, look for a reason for the behavior, perhaps a need for attention or even leadership tendencies, and address that issue. Communication with adults in the school setting should be encouraged, not discouraged.

RESPECT

Dictionary definitions of respect include phrases like noticing, considering with courtesy, and holding in high esteem. Use of the term *dissing* highlights the importance young people place on the respect they receive from one another and adults. Many of the best crisis avoidance techniques are really demonstrations of respect for the individual while maintaining one's self-respect. Interactions teachers have with their students on a daily basis can communicate respect or its opposite.

One of the most important components of respect is *privacy*. Speaking to students privately about missing homework, poor grades, or misbehavior not only shows respect on the part of the teacher, but it avoids identifying students as failures among peers. Unfortunately, some of the ostracism that takes place in classrooms is because the teachers themselves single out the same students over and over again for their failures.

Similar to the issue of privacy is that of *personal space*. This is not to suggest that school personnel do not have a right or even a responsibility to check student desks and lockers; however, explaining to students the reason why checks are important and carrying them out with a respect for privacy and personal property create a more positive school atmosphere.

Body language can also communicate a teacher's feelings for a student. A teacher who towers over a child with index finger wagging should expect negative feelings to build within that child. Confrontational stances, where the teacher squares off face to face with a student, contribute to battles of will, rather than to problem solving. Raised voices have a similar effect and may even suggest that the teacher is experiencing a loss of control rather than being able to influence or protect her students.

Making assumptions about a student's behavior or motivation creates frustration and anger, especially in students who may be trying to change long-term negative reputations. Saying that a student is not trying, could do better, or is making excuses creates a confrontational atmosphere. Teachers should always get accurate information before accusing students and should never identify a student by her negative behavior.

Calling a student a liar or saying she is lazy, rude, or selfish fosters the negative feelings and behavior of which crises are made. Giving the student the benefit of the doubt or at least keeping one's suspicions private is not being naïve. It shows awareness of the importance of fair and respectful attitudes in any environment. For an excellent review of ways to create a supportive classroom, see Brooks's chapter on creating nurturing classroom environments in *Best Practices in School Crisis Prevention and Intervention* (2002) published by the National Association of School Psychologists.

Since teachers are on the front line, they are in a good position to assess the interests and capabilities of their students. One sign of respect that a school as a whole can show students is to *cater to a wide variety of interests*. Most teachers know that not all students can play basketball or football, and some would not want to if they could. Teachers should advocate for music, art, theater, chess, and other activities that draw students of different types into the school community. Not all of these activities have to be competitive in nature. Contributing some time to these lower-profile activities can be a worthwhile contribution of the classroom teacher and one that enhances the respectful tone of the school.

Following one study of teacher style and its relationship to the behavior of students suspended for defiance of teacher authority, researchers concluded that even among this population, "teachers who consider relationships with students important for their classroom discipline are more likely to have greater trust and cooperation from students" (Gregory and Ripski, 2008, p. 349). They note that, "Even one supportive relationship with an adult at school can have significant positive effects on a student's school functioning" (p. 349).

SEEKING ASSISTANCE AND SUPPORT

A network of professional support is an important part of crisis prevention for the classroom teacher. The most fortunate teachers will function in an environment where such assistance is institutional and systemic. For example, many schools have formal teams in place to provide consultation to teachers. Team membership varies but is likely to include an administrator, a teacher trained to work with students who have special needs, a school psychologist, and perhaps a guidance counselor or social worker. Others, such as the school nurse or speech pathologist, may also be asked to attend team meetings if their expertise is required.

These teams go by a variety of titles, for example, child study, student assistance, or instructional support teams. Members may determine when or if a student should be referred for special assessment or intervention; however, the primary goal of these teams is to provide support and guidance to the classroom teacher. (In the last section of this book we will discuss how teachers can prepare for a referral to these teams and the role various members play.) Teachers should avail themselves of this service and not be intimidated by the team.

Teachers make decisions on a daily basis that have important implications for their students, and they should not have to make these decisions alone. The team can make suggestions for interventions they might try, provide a second opinion about the meaning of a student's classroom behaviors or writing, and generally make sure that teachers are not alone in the important task of educating their students.

Not all schools have teacher assistance teams. Others may have teaching teams, which are groups of teachers responsible for the same students. These teams can serve functions similar to those of child study teams in supporting the individual teacher and have the added benefit of each member knowing the students. The potential drawback, however, is that some members who do have good ideas may feel reluctant to share them unless asked for fear they will appear to be "one-upping" their colleagues; therefore, members of teaching teams have to make it clear that they would be pleased to take advice or suggestions.

Teams, like any group, will often have their own personalities and procedural habits. While the team concept has the potential to be a great source of support and assistance to teachers, some do become opportunities for focusing on failures of students and the limited resources of the school. However, if a sincere effort is made on the part of the members to fully participate, share ideas, and try interventions that are agreed upon, teams can be effective sources of professional support for teachers.

Formal teams are simply not available in some schools. Then, teachers must be creative in developing a support system. If there is a mentor teacher or lead teacher program available, they can provide help, new ideas, and an opportunity to share concerns. Failing those, the individual teacher must find at least one or two other teachers who can provide professional support. To be effective as a resource for professional development, these support groups, whether formal or informal, must provide information, suggestions, and resources, not just opportunities to ventilate frustration.

Some form of "buddy system" is also important in crisis management and prevention. There should be at least one other teacher, whose room is in close proximity to yours, who would be available to assist you, if necessary. This is especially helpful for teachers whose rooms are in more isolated parts of a building or in proximity to locations where conflicts are likely to take place, such as the cafeteria or a stairwell.

A communication system should be set up between the two of you so you can let one another know if assistance is necessary. (In some schools there may be someone other than a teacher designated as a contact person in these situations.) Modern technology makes it easier for teachers to stay in touch with the central office, other teachers, and administrators through cell phones, two-way radios, pagers, and intercoms. These forms of communication represent money well spent, even for the most financially challenged schools. If your school does not have such a system, work toward getting one and, in the meantime, consider providing your own cell phone or other communication system. (Be careful here. Cell phones are not appropriate under some conditions, and your school may have a policy with regard to their use. Investigate this thoroughly before proceeding.)

LAWS AND REGULATIONS

With all that new teachers have to do and learn, it is understandable that they may tend to focus most on what they need to know to function day to day; however, new teachers must make time to become familiar with laws and regulations that relate to low incidence, high consequence events. No teacher wants to have to find out how to handle a serious event while the event is unfolding. During times of stress, we are least likely to recall some vague procedure or remember where we put that list of things to do. Keys to effective use of laws and procedures in order of practice include the following:

- Carefully read all legal and procedural material you are given related to low incidence, high consequence issues when you are first employed by a new school district.

- Check with colleagues or an administrator to be sure you clearly understand the procedures and your role in carrying them out.
- Ask about procedures for any type of incident for which you have not received guidance.
- If the material is not in brief, easily accessible form, rewrite it.
- Keep one set of the brief form in a secure place at home and one in an easily accessible place in your classroom.
- Be sure to update your brief form whenever you receive notice of changes.

All teachers should be familiar with state laws in a minimum of the following areas:

- reporting child abuse and neglect
- bullying prevention
- discussing pregnancy, contraception, and abortion with students
- release of student information
- responsibility and self-protection issues when intervening in student fights
- responsibility and self-protection issues if assaulted by a student

All teachers should also be familiar with school system policy and procedures regarding all of the above, but also the following:

- handling student suicidal or homicidal threats
- carrying out in-class procedures in the event of a schoolwide crisis, for example, intruders, bomb threats, and natural disasters
- addressing threats from parents
- reacting to a student who runs from or is missing from class
- reporting/recording procedures following any incident

Advance preparation is extremely important to the effective and safe resolution of conflict in schools. For example, Fields (2002) strongly recommends that teachers become familiar with guidelines for their district and state regarding handling fights at school, because this is an area of legal liability, as well as physical risk. She suggests that educators utilize mental imagery in planning for how they will handle the various physical altercations that could occur in the school setting.

PROFESSIONAL DEVELOPMENT

In addition to colleague consultation and support, other methods for developing your skills in crisis prevention and intervention are in-service training and formal coursework. Most states require that teachers engage in postcredential learning experiences as a requirement of maintaining their teaching credential. Many larger school systems will offer their own courses to teachers or training through central education agencies. These training opportunities are often free to the teacher, with postcredential credits as an added bonus.

Most schools are required by their states to offer some form of continuing education to teachers. Unfortunately, these training options are often based on recent system changes that require the teacher to learn a new procedure or process while not necessarily learning new concepts or capabilities. While it is tempting to take advantage of the most convenient option, it is much more productive to develop an educational plan based on your career goals and learning needs.

For teachers who plan to specialize or have special interests in an academic area, the choices are obvious. For teachers whose interests are in social/emotional development of students, behavior management, or family-school relations, choices may not be so clear, and the options may be more limited. Plan ahead and explore the possibilities. Check into what is being offered at neighboring schools. Above all, keep your own individual learning needs and goals in mind, and don't do training that is irrelevant to those goals and needs unless required by your school.

Graduate Coursework

Graduate coursework is costly. Some districts may reimburse you for tuition, but many will not. Individual courses may not be applied to a full graduate degree should you eventually decide to apply for one. Thus, even more than with continuing education, you must plan carefully before taking graduate courses. On the plus side, many colleges and universities now offer courses online, and you will have a much wider range of choices than if you only take continuing education courses from your school system. You will make contacts with specialists in your area of interest and fellow students who share that interest.

When choosing graduate courses, don't limit yourself to just departments of education. Consider courses in psychology, educational psychology, special education, and sociology. In some colleges and universities, these will be separate departments. In others, they will be grouped together. Go to the course catalog and explore.

OUTSIDE AGENCIES

Several local, state, and national organizations offer training in crisis prevention and intervention that relates to schools. What is best will depend on what you want to learn. Local suicide prevention, mental health, and abuse prevention agencies train volunteers to work hotlines. These skills can translate into those required in assisting stressed students in schools. Four well-known national organizations that offer training are the International Red Cross, Crisis Prevention Institute, National Association of School Psychologists, and Federal Emergency Management Agency.

The International Red Cross

The International Red Cross offers a wide range of courses in CPR and first aid, as well as disaster preparedness. Volunteers offering to serve in disaster services are subject to screening and background checks. Training of volunteers is free and ranges from a general course in introduction to disaster services to more specific courses, such as foundations of disaster mental health and psychological first aid (American Red Cross of the Greater Lehigh Valley, 2010).

The Crisis Prevention Institute

The Crisis Prevention Institute (CPI) has been training educators and other public service providers in crisis prevention and intervention for more than 30 years. Emphasis is on preventing and easing confrontation between students (or clients) and staff through "understanding effective communication and human physiology during aggressive moments" (Crisis Prevention Institute, 2010).

The CPI is one of the few organizations offering physical crisis intervention training. There is a substantial fee, but schools can send one person to be trained as a trainer and that person can come back and train others.

The National Association of School Psychologists

The PREPaRE program of the National Association of School Psychologists (NASP) is specifically designed for crisis prevention and intervention in schools. PREPaRE stands for Prevent (and prepare for psychological trauma), Reaffirm (physical health and perceptions of security and safety), Evaluate (psychological trauma risk), Provide (interventions) and Respond (to psychological needs), and Examine (the effectiveness of crisis prevention and intervention) (National Association of School Psychologists, 2009).

While the program is sponsored by an association of school psychologists, the training is intended for all educators. The cost for training, either for schools or any one individual, is much less than that of the CPI. Emphasis is on awareness of national crisis management procedures, crisis team development and management, prevention of school crises, and postvention. The authors bring the benefit of personal involvement in major school crises of the past and in-depth research into best practices in school crisis management, including natural disasters, suicide, violence, and student/staff death.

Two-day-long workshops make up the basic training. (There are additional requirements for those who wish to become trainers.) Workshop 1 addresses prevention and preparedness, specifically the school crisis team. Workshop 2 addresses crisis intervention and recovery, specifically the role of the school-based mental health professional. Trainings are offered throughout the country and at the yearly NASP conference. Summer trainings are also usually offered. As more trainers are trained, availability of the service will increase. The most efficient way to obtain training is to have your school system request a trainer from NASP.

The Federal Emergency Management Agency

The Federal Emergency Management Institute, part of the Federal Emergency Management Agency (FEMA), offers several courses in the National Incident Management System and Incident Command System (see chapter 11). For information go to the FEMA website, www.training.fema.gov/emiweb/is/.

SUMMARY

In this chapter, we have emphasized the importance of advance planning and a supportive environment in preventing crisis events and minimizing their impact. Awareness and active involvement of the classroom teacher is a key piece of prevention. To be most effective, the teacher should be aware of state regulations and school district procedures but also mindful of his or her own need for support and assistance from other professionals. Options for formal professional development were also discussed.

CHAPTER 10

Prevention Techniques for Use in the Classroom

> Schools possess both the capacity and human resources to mobilize many of the protective processes believed to ameliorate risk.
>
> —Doll and Lyon, 1998, p. 357

Teachers should focus primarily on the academic advancement of their students. Children and youth are in school to learn. In this age of accountability, high stakes testing, and financial difficulties, schools must have students actively engaged in academic pursuits during most of the time they are in school. Academic success also contributes to mental health, and academic failure enhances the risk of adjustment problems for children and youth.

However, when any group of people is together over long periods of time, relationship and management issues emerge. If the group is made up of people at various levels of maturity, cognitive ability, and background, as in schools, these relationship issues can be significant. The wise teacher will have methods for managing not only the classroom routine but the relationship issues that emerge among students. These techniques are not therapy. They are ways of preventing student behavior from interfering with the job at hand, which is teaching and learning.

Federal and state regulations, as well as ethical practice, require that the methods used be based on evidence of effectiveness. The potential for profiteering and bandwagon effects makes it exceedingly important that educators be careful consumers as they match attempts to assist students with needs shown.

Several websites devoted to effective practice are available. For just two examples, see www.cdc.gov/healthyyouth/index.htm, a link of the Centers for Disease Control, and www.nrepp.samhsa.gov/, a national registry of evidence-based programs and practices. What follows is a general review of topics and programs of which teachers should be aware as they make decisions about techniques to use in classrooms.

AFFECTIVE/CHARACTER EDUCATION

One method that has been tried to improve human relations in the classroom, as well as later in life, is affective/character education. Here the use if this term means an instructional program intended to enhance knowledge about emotions, behaviors, or values to improve the adjustment of children or youth. The concept of affective education is not new. Those of you who have been in the field for a while may remember DUSO (Developing Understanding of Self and Others, Dinkmeyer, 1970, 1982), which was popular in the 1970s and 1980s. This is a specific curriculum, complete with a kit of materials, designed to help students learn more about emotions and how their behavior affects others. A more recent example would be Project DARE (Drug Abuse Resistance Education), intended to help students learn techniques for handling peer pressure to engage in substance abuse.

Some affective education programs have had mixed results, in part because they address issues only loosely related to healthy behavior. Programs intended to enhance self-esteem are one example. The concept of self-esteem is complex. Whether improvement of self-esteem alone leads to prosocial behavior, or even better mental health, has not been clearly demonstrated. That lower self-esteem may be correlated with emotional problems does not necessarily mean that improvement in self-esteem prevents these problems; therefore, teachers are advised to thoroughly research any programs in affective/character education that they consider for use in their classrooms.

One must have evidence, not only that the program is effective in teaching the concept, but that the concept itself is actually related to better adjustment for students. A common sense connection is not sufficient here. These programs often consume a great deal of educational time. Even if they are only done in individual classrooms, and not schoolwide, they take up valuable resources, such as money and space. DARE, for example, has been reported to cost three quarters of a billion dollars annually, with many researchers finding it to be largely ineffective (Thombs, 2000; West and O'Neal, 2004). In many instances, resources would be better spent on well-supported interventions for students known to be at risk.

Affective/character education programs that are most effective will teach alternative behaviors to those the program is intended to change, help students monitor their own behavior, provide examples of how the alternative behavior works and why, and show relevance to the student audience being targeted. Just being aware of a concept does not necessarily lead to behavior change. For example, students may learn the symptoms of depression. If they never discuss what to do if they see signs of depression in themselves or others, protective behaviors are unlikely to develop.

A PROBLEM-SOLVING ORIENTATION

Some of the most effective behavior and classroom management procedures are those that teach problem-solving and social skills and give students the opportunity to discuss real-world situations. These techniques are often known as cognitive-behavioral interventions, cognitive because they target the student's thinking and judgment, and behavioral because improved problem-solving skills are intended to change student behavior in positive ways. Cognitive behavioral programs have several distinguishing characteristics that make them appropriate for use in schools, including the following:

- Students learn about the connection between thoughts, feelings, and behavior.
- Students are asked to think before they act.
- Students are taught to brainstorm several solutions to a problem.
- Students practice evaluating solutions before they choose one.
- Students reward themselves for appropriate behavior.

Teachers can utilize these techniques in the everyday life of the classroom by instructing students about the previously mentioned characteristics and then applying them to those "teaching moments" when classmates are arguing, teasing, or acting out. The teacher can model effective problem solving by verbally going through relevant steps and reflecting on his or her own problem-solving behaviors.

There are a number of packaged programs that make it easier for teachers to teach and model the appropriate skills. Most of these allow the teacher to use all or only some of the program and include visuals for use in the classroom. These visuals serve to remind students to stop, think, and problem solve.

One well-known cognitive behavior program is *I Can Problem Solve (ICPS)*, by Myrna Shure (2001). This program has been evolving for more than 30 years and has a substantial research base (Aberson and Shure, 2002). Published packages are available for preschool through the elementary grades that have students brainstorm and evaluate solutions to common problems they face, like what to do about conflict on the playground or if one is being teased.

Another similar program is *Cognitive Behavioral Therapy for Impulsive Children* (Kendall and Braswell, 1993). This process can be used in academic as well as social situations and requires students to self-instruct by asking themselves what they are supposed to do, reviewing the possible alternative behaviors, choosing an answer, and evaluating their response. The teacher models the behavior and self-instructs out loud, then self instructs softly, and then silently. The student follows the same steps. The student is being taught to focus, think in an organized fashion, evaluate his or her performance, and self reward or correct. This procedure is likely to be especially helpful to children with attention problems.

Three problem-solving/social skills curricula cited by the Virginia Department of Health as representing best practice in violence prevention are PATHS (Promoting Alternative Thinking Strategies), the Second Step Violence Prevention Curriculum, and The Good Behavior Game. PATHS is an extensive elementary curriculum including lessons in self-control, feelings/relationships, and problem solving (Kam, Greenberg, and Kusche, 2004; Kusche and Greenberg, 1994; Seifer, Gouley, Miller, and Zakriski, 2004). Materials include visuals and teacher manuals. This program offers in-depth training for staff and is to be utilized over extended periods of time.

The Second Step Violence Prevention Curriculum, for children in preschool through junior high, teaches attitude and behavior change through modeling, rehearsal, and role-play. Lessons are taught by classroom teachers in stress management, problem solving, and what is described by researchers of the program as "perspective taking" (Taub, 2001; Van Schoiack-Edstrom, Frey, and Beland, 2002).

The Good Behavior Game is a behavior management technique that includes specific descriptions of desirable behaviors, behaviors that interfere with learning and positive behavioral outcomes (called fouls), and examples of each that children can understand. Students are divided into teams that compete to see which group can attain the most desired behaviors with the least number of fouls. Various types of rewards can be utilized (Embry, 2002).

While there are a number of published problem-solving programs for use in the classroom, it is possible to adopt a problem-solving orientation to behavior and relationship management in your class without the benefit of a packaged program. Problem-solving approaches require an emphasis on identification of patterns of behavior and the generation of alternative behaviors that are likely to achieve a better outcome than the behavior in which the student is currently engaging.

Reality Check

At least three days per week, Albert comes to school without his homework. When it is time to turn it in, he becomes visibly anxious. Each day his teacher asks for his homework, and Albert says he can't find it. Mrs. Hengle, his third grade teacher, tells him he is expected to have his homework done. He often makes an excuse, which Mrs. Hengle usually says is not a good reason. Albert then sulks and throws his books on the floor or otherwise shows his temper to Mrs. Hengle. Mrs. Hengle reacts by sending Albert to time out or discussing his outbursts with him after the lesson.

With a problem-solving approach, Mrs. Hengle would first identify the behavior pattern, in this case, that the negative behavior takes place when homework is to be turned in. Second, she would focus not on

Table 10.1.   Traditional Methods versus Problem-Solving Techniques

Traditional Methods	Problem-Solving Techniques
Teacher places emphasis on the child's behavior	Teachers places emphasis on the problem to be solved
Teacher provides consequences	Teacher teaches skills
Teacher tries different methods to change student's behavior	Student tries different methods to change his or her own behavior
Teacher rewards appropriate behavior	Student self-rewards (teacher may also reward)

Albert's outbursts, but on the issue that seems to lead to the outbursts, which is the failure to turn in homework. Third, with Albert's assistance, she would generate some alternatives to the way he is handling the current homework situation. Perhaps he needs to do homework in his after-school day care setting, for example.

With the help of Mrs. Hengle, Albert would generate some alternatives and choose one to try. Mrs. Hengle would then help Albert evaluate the success of the behavior he chose, knowing that she may have to help him choose another if the first was unsuccessful. When Albert is successful in turning in his homework, she would remind him of how they agreed he would self-reward, perhaps by telling himself what a good job he has done.

In other situations, teachers may have to actually teach an alternative behavior. For example, if students are fighting over a toy on the playground, the kindergarten teacher may take advantage of that "teaching moment" and show them how to take turns. Problem-solving techniques differ from some of the more traditional methods teachers use to foster behavior change in the ways detailed in table 10.1.

CLASS MEETINGS

The use of class meetings to facilitate relationships in the classroom is related, in part, to the popularity of group treatment for emotional difficulties in the 1960s and 1970s. The basic premise, rooted in a history of psychotherapy too extensive to cover here, was that issues and emotions that go unaired will intensify and that releasing emotion and addressing concerns is important to mental health. Determining whether this is, in fact, so is difficult. But, attempts have been made to take some of what was known in the field of clinical psychology and apply it to school relationship and behavior problems.

Many different approaches to class meetings are described in the literature. Because there are so many different ways meetings can be carried out, it is impossible to make a general statement about whether the technique is effective as a form of relationship management in the classroom. Most approaches focus on giving students the opportunity to speak and be heard, creating an accepting environment for all students, and developing a plan for addressing problems that arise in the classroom. All of these are important and worthy goals for any classroom teacher.

The use of classroom meetings is not without its challenges. First, meetings take time. Second, even the best behavior manager will find it difficult to keep the entire class focused on the topics at hand, especially when classes in some schools still have 30 students or more. Third, unpredicted topics sometimes arise, requiring the teacher to "think on her feet" about a sensitive issue. This can be particularly difficult for the new teacher. Of course, these factors can be managed. Teachers who would like to learn more about this approach should refer to *Crisis Counseling for a Quality School Community* by Palmatier (1998). Palmatier provides specific guidelines from professionals with a long history of perfecting and researching this technique.

Some programs include both group meetings and curricula for the development of specific social skills. One such program is SkillStreaming (Goldstein, Sprafkin, Gershaw, and Klein, 1984; McGinnis and Goldstein, 1990a, 1990b). SkillStreaming programs are available for every age level and can be tailored for use with students who have disabilities. The program involves instruction and then practice through role-playing of different social skills. Teachers do not have to teach all of the skills and can pick the aspects of the program that seem most relevant to their situation.

Class meetings are also part of the Olweus Bullying Prevention Program (Olweus et al., 2003). Formal training to use the program is likely to enhance the teacher's confidence in handling class meetings; however, elementary school teachers could learn about the program through reading on their own and use some of the ideas in meetings with their class. The use of class meetings is more problematic for teachers at the secondary level under usual circumstances, because students change classes, and their harassment, bullying, and ostracizing issues are more complex. Group meetings, should they be the technique of choice, are probably best carried out by a school psychologist or guidance counselor in secondary schools.

READING/CONTENT CURRICULUM

Using reading to improve student adjustment or behavior, sometimes called bibliotherapy, incorporates stories, books, and literature to help students reflect on life problems. In spite of the term, the process is not therapy per se, although it is a technique that can be used by psychotherapists. It is especially applicable to children because it allows them to discuss important, perhaps emotionally laden issues, from a distance. The person in the story is not them, so there is a bit of distance from the situation.

Another reason this approach is useful in schools is that students can be given the opportunity to consider a situation without revealing personal or family information. A story about a family who loses all of their belongings in a hurricane, for example, allows students to discuss how people might feel when that happens. If people in a book can feel bad, be sad, work together, and then recover, those must be "okay" and possible things to feel and do. When classmates respond warmly to the person in the story, anyone in the class who has been in a similar situation is supported.

Books and stories can also serve to create empathy for others. For example, if too much teasing has been taking place in the class, the teacher may want to have the class read a story about someone who has been teased. This may make it easier for the students to think about how their behavior could cause someone else to feel. Of course, this approach is somewhat indirect and would not be appropriate for more serious classroom management problems.

Many publishers of children's books and guidance materials offer a variety of titles to choose from if you would like to use this technique to enhance classroom management. Your school guidance counselor should also have appropriate books. However, if the issues addressed are controversial, it is advisable to consult with your school administration before using a particular book or story. The additional reading list in appendix A includes books to be read with and to children that should foster discussion of many of the difficult situations they may face.

The school's curriculum in various content areas also provides a multitude of opportunities for students to learn about emotions, crisis events, and the human circumstances that surround them. A study of the Civil War can incorporate the ethical and moral issues confronting generals and presidents. The challenges of leadership, the presence of peer pressure throughout the various stages of life, and ways of coping with stress can all be part of a study of leaders in any context. Some authors suggest that the concepts of cooperation, responsibility, commitment, self-control, and tolerance be integrated and emphasized in various aspects of the curriculum (McLaughlin, Kubick, and Lewis, 2002). (For ideas on how to integrate character issues into English classes, see Gilness, 2003.)

The curriculum can also be utilized to help students reflect on a crisis that has taken place and learn from it. Using subject content in this way helps students see the role of intellect and knowledge in managing crisis situations and gives them an element of hope and control (Pitcher and Poland, 1992). If, for example, a community has experienced a major hurricane, once school reopens, there are ways that the hurricanes can be incorporated into student learning experiences at every grade level, for example, in the following ways:

Elementary
  Explore what causes hurricanes.
  Study where hurricanes are most common and why.
  Learn how hurricanes are predicted.
  Find out how people can protect themselves from hurricanes.
  Study the Red Cross and how they help people.
Middle School
  Study scientific aspects of weather prediction.
  Explore careers connected to weather, crisis management, and
    health care.

Discuss the effects of stress on communities, families, and schools.
Study crises in literature or history. (Greenstone and Leviton, 2002)
High School
Study science related to hurricanes and weather prediction.
Explore the psychology of crisis reactions and interventions.
Learn about the challenges of crisis management organizations.
Find out about the issues related to community voluntarism.
Learn leadership skills and crisis management.
Study the media and how they address crises.
Discuss the journalistic challenges of reporting crisis events.
(Greenstone and Leviton, 2002)

FAMILY-SCHOOL RELATIONS

There is an abundance of research suggesting that parent involvement in the education of their children leads to more positive learning outcomes (Bowman, 1994; Christenson and Sheridan, 2001; Cronin, Slade, Bechtel, and Anderson, 1992). There are parents who will work well with the school regardless of the techniques educators use to involve them. There are, of course, a few who will not cooperate with the school no matter how they are approached. Many, however, are somewhere in the middle. So, the wise teacher will learn several different methods of engaging parents.

It is easier to build successful family-school relations when the process is valued districtwide; however, a school's lack of emphasis in this area, or even failure, does not necessarily mean any one teacher cannot build successful parent relationships. The following teacher behaviors set a positive tone:

- Communicate with parents about positive student performance, not just when there is a problem.
- Periodically inform parents of whole-class activities.
- If you do have a problem to discuss with parents, be prepared to contribute suggestions for possible solutions. Don't expect the solution to come only from them.

- Be open to parents' suggestions for meeting their child's needs.
- Be prepared to function as a professional consultant regarding a variety of school services and help parents access them.
- Be prepared to function as a professional consultant to parents whose children are having academic problems.
- Learn the common family characteristics of the multicultural groups with which you work.
- Learn the common characteristics of families with special needs, such as those of substance abusers, those who have a child with a disability, single-parent families, and low income families.

It should be clear from these recommendations that, ideally, the teacher is in a role of professional support to the parent. This is the exact opposite of the model where the teacher complains to the parent about a child's behavior or performance and expects the parent to take care of the problem. Parents may have suggestions, and their ideas should be considered and adopted when helpful; however, the teacher is the professional educator.

As a school psychologist, I have frequently heard parents say, "The school says he isn't doing his work. They want me to do something about it. They're the educators. If they don't know what to do, how should I?" Sometimes this is seen as a parent shirking responsibility. Maybe sometimes it is; however, perhaps they really don't know what to do. Many uncomplicated, well-researched interventions are covered in educational psychology classes all teachers take. Teachers should dig back into that training and use it to help parents.

The Parent-Teacher Conference

Few teachers receive training in parent conferencing, one of the most important activities in which they engage with regard to family-school relations. Parent conferences have three phases. Unfortunately, we sometimes lose parental support during the first phase, before they even get through the school door. Important factors to consider at each phase of the parent conference are listed in the following sections.

Phase I: Planning and Scheduling

Effective actions that should be taken during the planning and scheduling phase include the following:

- *Ensure adequate time for each conference.* Teachers usually know which children will take more time to discuss but are often bound by a schoolwide schedule that gives 20 minutes per parent regardless of the circumstances. Try to modify this policy so that sufficient time is given, when it is warranted.
- *Offer evening or Saturday conference times when student issues are significant and parents cannot or will not come during the week.* Again, this is often a school policy issue; however, a lack of flexibility in regard to scheduling at a time when so many parents work is unproductive. Be sure meeting places are safe and accessible.
- *Offer conference times outside the regular schedule when children are having difficulty.* Precious time can be lost while we wait for the fixed district conference period.
- *Be open to and encourage attendance by parental support figures who may have influence on the family, such as ministers and father or mother figures not married to the parent.* This is especially important in multicultural groups where extended family members or pastors may have significant influence on children. Of course, parents must want these other individuals to attend.
- *Outline the purpose of the conference and topics to be discussed at the time that the appointment is arranged.* Giving parents suggestions of how they might prepare for the conference and telling them what they will be asked and the type of information they will be given empowers them to be full partners.

Phase II: The Meeting

In phase II, the meeting phase, the following should be done to use the allotted meeting time most wisely:

- *After welcoming and briefly hosting the parent, begin the meeting by stating the reason for the conference, the amount of time allot-*

ted, and what will be discussed. Parents should be given a brief outline of what will be discussed during the conference.

- *Ask the parent what topics he or she would like to discuss.* This again emphasizes that the meeting is an opportunity for two-way communication. If all the teacher hopes to do is tell the parent how the child is performing, that can be done with a written report. Face-to-face meetings should foster communication.
- *If the parent has a pressing issue, begin with that.* Address the issue first, if appropriate. If it should wait until a later point in the conference, promise to cover it then.
- *Begin your part of the communication with at least one specific and true strength of the child, and then follow with areas that need improvement, if necessary.* This starts the conference off on a positive note.
- *Be clear in communication about the child's strengths and needs.* The conference is not a social situation where we avoid unpleasant topics. Parents who do not get clear messages at the conference will be blindsided by poor grades.
- *Do not come to the conference armed with a long list of examples to prove your point about how poorly the child is behaving or performing.* This alienates parents and seems to suggest that your professional judgment is not sufficient to make your case. State your concerns. If the parent asks for specific examples, provide one or two.
- *Do not generalize the personality of the child from a behavior.* For example, "When John comes in from recess, he often complains that the other students will not let him play with them" is an appropriate statement. "John doesn't know how to get along with other children" is not, unless you can be sure that is the reason the other children are not playing with him.
- *Keep the conference moving so all important topics get covered.* It is important to take advantage of the opportunity and touch on all issues rather than dwelling on just one.
- *End the feedback part of the conference with another positive comment about the child (again, be sure it is true).* This maintains a positive tone and reiterates that the teacher is not there to attack the parent or child.

- *Always come up with at least one plan and a backup (in case the first is not successful) for any problem addressed.* Doing so will avoid the need to meet again to set up a plan.
- *Summarize at the end of the conference by reviewing the main points covered, the plan, and who will do what by what time.* Outlining what has been discussed is a good reminder to both the teacher and the parent what has been accomplished and what actions need to be taken moving forward.
- *Be sure to identify effective methods of follow-up communication, including e-mail, home phone, cell phone, and so forth.* Finding out how different parents prefer to communicate improves the odds that effective communication will occur.

Phase III: Follow-Up

During the follow-up phase, the following are helpful in maintaining open lines of communication with parents:

- *Do what you said you would do in a timely fashion.* If the teacher follows through on what he or she promised to do, the parents are more likely to do the same.
- *If you were responsible for contacting other school personnel, be sure they got back to the parent.* This is an important step in maintaining the line of communication you have worked hard to establish.
- *If the parent does not do what he/she was to do in a timely fashion, contact quickly and don't wait.* The conference time was time wasted if follow-up does not take place.

One conference issue that frequently arises with those who teach in a multicultural setting is the language barrier. In spite of the inconvenience and complexity of locating interpreters, school personnel should avoid having children interpret for their parents. This upsets the natural order of families where parents are meant to be in charge and children are given care.

Schools that allow children to interpret give the massage that parents are less than competent and need to be led and assisted by their children. Interpreter children can also become privy to unnecessary information about their siblings. This also leads to an imbalance of influence where some children are parentified, that is, given an inappropriate responsibility for their age and position in the family, and others are stigmatized as "problem children."

Advance planning for family-school communication is important if language is an issue. In larger metropolitan areas, there are often support organizations that can provide an interpreter if given enough notice. Parents may have someone in mind themselves. They might be invited to bring a trusted adult to the conference. In any event, providing interpreters is not helpful if all conference arrangements were sent home in English. Again, advance planning should involve conference notices and options for interpreters being sent home in the family's native language.

ELECTRONIC COMMUNICATION

We all know that technology has its benefits and downfalls. Electronic communication certainly makes parent-teacher contact easier. Contact can be more frequent, and problems that otherwise would have waited for attention until they got much worse can be addressed in a timely fashion. However, there are some concerns related to electronic communication of which the teacher must be aware.

Not all situations can be appropriately addressed electronically. There is still a place for face-to-face communication. Sensitive issues are rarely handled adequately by electronic means. Attempts to handle these matters in such a way can lead to misunderstandings and emotional overreaction, both of which will interfere with later attempts to work things out.

Teachers should be careful to not leave the choice of communication method completely to the parent. You are the education professional. If you think a meeting is needed, do not communicate by e-mail just because it is more convenient for the parent. Beware of the tendency to communicate electronically because you don't want to encounter the difficulties presented by face-to-face communication. Interacting with parents is part of your job, and you must master the skills needed to do it effectively.

Other issues are lack of confidentiality and the permanence of a written statement. Think carefully before you write. Are you writing something that should not be in the hands of the family babysitter, the visiting grandparent, or the child herself? Could what you have written be easily misinterpreted if read only on its own, without awareness of the context? Are you writing in the heat of the moment? Might your message sound impatient or unfeeling? Are you aware of and following school policy with regard to electronic communication?

GRADING

With the variety of grading systems currently used in schools and the large number of tests given at state and local levels, it is a wise parent, indeed, who can understand what it all means. This is another place where the teacher can assist the parent and thereby improve relations between parent and school. With rubrics, portfolios, percentile rankings, cut-off scores, and grade equivalents, parents will often go to the person they know and trust, the classroom teacher, to get it all figured out.

Be prepared and willing to help, and they are likely to be very grateful. Provide clear-cut guidelines to students and parents on how your students will be graded in class. This is best done by giving them a list of standards you will use when you grade work. Advance planning and communication should cut down on parent questions regarding grading; however, it is important to be willing to discuss your grading procedures and not take a defensive posture if your grades are questioned.

SCHOOLWIDE PROGRAMS

While you would probably want to have the blessing of your administrator before using them, most of the prevention techniques above, if not an entire program, can be implemented by a single classroom teacher in one classroom; however, there are a number of schoolwide programs, some of which are experimental, and some of which are well-supported, that can affect school climate.

If your school is using one of these techniques, you should learn the most effective ways of supporting it in your classroom. No program will effectively change student behavior if it is not brought to the level of everyday interaction in the classroom. Similarly, a schoolwide program that is not working for the students in your classroom may have significant flaws that should be pointed out to the administration.

In a thorough article addressing what helps create resilience in children, Doll and Lyon (1998) emphasize the key role of schools. They point out that schools have a special opportunity to develop student strengths because they "represent one of the most potentially protective environments, encouraging the development of good problem-solving skills, individual talents and other productive activities, and social competence" (p. 357). This is done, they argue, through a school culture that provides the emotional supports students need and fosters what we know is related to student resilience, including relationships with positive adult models, academic success, and a variety of school activities that foster a connection with the organization (Doll and Lyon, 1998).

Some schoolwide programs are theoretical, that is, they provide a way of looking at what children need but are open ended with regard to ways the school can meet these needs. Others, such as the Olweus Bullying Prevention Program, are prescriptive, with manuals and guidelines for what educators should do and how.

One that provides a theoretical approach is the Developmental Assets Framework (see Paine and Paine in Shinn, Walker, and Stoner, *Interventions for Academic and Behavior Problems II* [2002] for a review). This program talks about the most important assets within children and in their environments for fostering healthy adjustment. There are a variety of ways schools can enhance these assets.

A schoolwide approach that has gotten a good deal of attention in the last few years is *Positive Behavior Support* (PBS). (Additional related terms you will see are *Positive Behavioral Interventions and Supports* and *Schoolwide Positive Behavioral Support*.) Key concepts of PBS are clear behavioral expectations stated in positive terms, instruction in appropriate behavior, known and clear consequences for behavior, and monitoring and data gathering that influence decision making. PBS is often delivered in the context of a three-tiered system that addresses the behavioral needs of all students, those at risk, and those who have demonstrated significant difficulty, with different levels and types of techniques.

For an overview of PBS and other schoolwide programs designed to prevent school violence, including character education, conflict resolution, bullying prevention, and partnering with families, see *Transforming School Mental Health Services*, by Doll and Cummings (2008), or Osher, Dwyer, and Jackson's (2004) *Safe, Supportive, and Successful Schools: Step by Step*. For specifics on PBS, go to www.pbis.org.

Safe, Supportive, and Successful Schools contains checklists schools can use to evaluate their environments with regard to prevention, intervention, and goal setting. In any approach adopted to improve school climate, it is important that the school and community work together, that student involvement be encouraged, and that there be sensitivity to diversity and respect for all students (McLaughlin, Kubick, and Lewis, 2002).

SUMMARY

In this chapter, we discussed the most effective techniques for fostering healthy relationships in the classroom, including good teaching, respect for students and families, and a problem-solving approach for issues that do arise. There are many published programs available to help teachers manage behavior and student relationships in the classroom. Because not all are effective, teachers must be wise consumers. Family-school relations begin with the classroom teacher, so you must use your training in behavior management, child development, and assessment and your knowledge of schools to guide parents through the system and help them access the supports they and their children need.

CHAPTER 11

Crisis Response Teams

A comprehensive plan that includes crisis preparedness and crisis response procedures is the foundation of a safe school.

—Paine, 2002, p. 1,017

While once simply considered a good idea, school crisis response teams are now a requirement for any education agency receiving federal funding. The Safe and Drug Free Schools and Communities Act requires education agencies receiving their funds to

have a plan for keeping their schools safe and drug free that includes appropriate and effective discipline policies, security procedures, prevention activities, as well as a student code of conduct and emergency management plan for responding to violent and traumatic events on school grounds. (U.S. Department of Education, 2006a, p. 1)

School districts that receive federal emergency preparedness funds are also required to utilize the National Incident Management System (NIMS). NIMS is primarily an organizational and coordination system for the management of crisis situations among federal, state, and local agencies. Those complying with NIMS requirements receive training and institute an Incident Command System that identifies the roles and responsibilities at different levels of the management system.

NIMS reminds districts that they must plan for a crisis in the following ways: command and management (acting as primary manager and decision maker), preparedness, resource management, communication and information management, supporting technologies, and ongoing management and maintenance (U.S. Department of Education, 2006b). The needs of those with disabilities must also be addressed in the plan.

School crisis prevention and intervention teams do not just address extreme and low-incidence events like school shootings or terrorist attacks. Paine (2002) notes that in 10 years, the Springfield School District in Springfield, Oregon (where Kip Kinkel killed his parents and two students), experienced the deaths of 24 students, 4 teachers, and 8 other staff members, not counting the Kinkel tragedy. This is for a district of only 11,000 students.

Since the time when Springfield and many other districts experienced these traumatic events, we have learned a lot about school crises; however, there is a great deal more to learn. This is an evolving area of research and application with a large amount of uncertainty still remaining. It is clear that crisis response teams, consisting of a cross section of school personnel, have an important role to play in enhancing the coping and adjustment of students and staff when tragedy strikes. Teams can be community-based, systemwide, or at the school level. Many school systems have a combination of all three. A crisis response team at any level must do a minimum of the following:

- develop a crisis intervention plan that lays out the procedures to be followed during a variety of crisis events
- identify those who will participate in crisis intervention
- specify the role of each participant in crisis intervention
- ensure that all of those likely to be involved in a crisis are aware of the plan
- plan for the training of team members and school personnel

COMMUNITY-BASED TEAMS

Communities are expected to have plans for coping with a variety of crisis events. Those for natural disasters have been in place for years and usually include designation of shelter sites; evacuation procedures; and information for the community on what to have on hand, for example, bottled water, batteries, and so forth. Schools have frequently had a role in these communitywide plans, and many schools are designated shelter areas; however, it is only in the last several years that events that might take place at the school have become the focus of communitywide plans.

Communitywide crisis intervention plans rarely involve the classroom teacher unless he or she is also a first responder, a volunteer firefighter, for example. Communitywide teams usually include representatives from government agencies, law enforcement, emergency services, the medical/mental health community, and the clergy. School crisis planners should be aware of what is in the communitywide plan and incorporate that plan into their own preparations. Schools should do the following when developing a communitywide plan:

- establish a communication system for notifying first responders of a school incident
- facilitate communication between primary crisis players in the community, including law enforcement and mental health and medical personnel, regarding their interaction with the schools
- assess resource allocation on a regular basis to ensure adequacy
- ensure that all parties have developed plans in their area of specialization that include school-related crises

While community crisis response plans include schools, school personnel themselves are responsible for the specifics of planning for a school crisis. Large districts should have multilevel plans and roles starting at the system level, perhaps moving to a unit that includes several schools in a geographical area, and, finally, a building-level plan and team. Smaller districts, of course, will not need a multilevel format and may have only one team with a number of different roles. Responsibilities of teams at various levels are discussed in the following section, but keep in mind that in a district with one team, all roles are to be played by that team, perhaps with community support.

SYSTEMWIDE TEAMS

All school systems should have a systemwide crisis intervention plan. These plans provide consistency and continuity across schools within the system. Systemwide teams should plan for the aspects of crisis intervention that would be the same regardless of the location of the school or age of the students.

In an excellent book devoted to the effective development and functioning of school crisis response teams, Brock, Sandoval, and Lewis (2001) discuss the importance of the careful selection of team members. Although teams that are too large can be unwieldy, it is important to include not only those who will assist with such direct intervention plans as emergency and mental health personnel, but those who facilitate management, for example, media specialists and teachers. Some of the responsibilities of a systemwide team are to do the following:

- establish procedures for handling specific crises, including bomb threats, suspicious strangers in the building, or events that prevent students from leaving the building
- identify who will fill such specific districtwide roles as incident commander and media specialist
- develop procedures for communicating with parents
- arrange contract agreements with members of the community or agencies that might assist in a large-scale intervention
- develop a communication system among key leaders during a crisis
- provide resources for computers, separate phone lines, cell phones, pagers, and other communication devices
- establish requirements for individual building crisis intervention plans
- print the districtwide crisis intervention plan in a formal complete form and in a brief user-friendly format
- update the school board on the status of the crisis plan on a regular basis
- develop a plan for emergency training exercises
- establish in-service opportunities and practice sessions for crisis planners and interveners

BUILDING-LEVEL TEAMS

In smaller districts, systemwide teams may function as interveners in individual buildings. In larger districts, building-level teams are essential due to the importance of having interveners who know school personnel, the students, and the community, as well as the physical plant of any individual school. Some of the responsibilities of the building level team are to do the following:

- ensure that building personnel are aware of relevant aspects of the districtwide crisis plan
- provide user friendly copies of the plan to each teacher and administrator
- organize the practice of crisis intervention procedures as needed
- establish communication procedures for the school, for example, procedures for informing teachers to go into lockdown
- develop procedures for their own functioning, including a process for reaching parties who are out of the building
- carry out crisis interventions within the school
- assess the degree of need for outside assistance once a crisis occurs
- locate safe sites near the school for circumstances requiring that students leave the building
- develop crisis boxes or materials to be available to each classroom teacher in a crisis event
- identify those who will carry out direct interventions

THE TEACHER AS A MEMBER OF THE CRISIS RESPONSE TEAM

Teachers can and do participate in crisis response teams. Not everyone has the temperament or desire to be part of these groups, but many teachers have the potential to be key players. They know the students, staff, buildings, and communities best and have training in child development and educational psychology; however, this new function may require thinking and behavior somewhat different from that of the teacher's traditional role.

The Role Shift

One of the greatest challenges to the teacher who is a member of the crisis response team is the role shift that is required. In many school systems, classroom teachers are not traditionally in the role of decision maker. They are more often participants in a schoolwide plan rather than being the plan makers; however, the teacher's role on the crisis response team is a vital one. One of the things we know to be true of crisis intervention is that it is best done by those who know the target community. People respond better to one of their own, someone who knows who is likely to be most vulnerable, where the resources are, and how to access those resources. This role is best served by the experienced teacher, not one who is new to the field of education or the school.

As a member of the crisis response team, one of the teacher's primary responsibilities is to help ensure that the team's planning is realistic with regard to the needs of the school. Physical plant, staff development, scheduling, and personnel and financial resources should be considered; therefore, crisis intervention plans from other schools and communities can and should be reviewed but can never be substituted for a plan designed for a specific school.

Teachers can also assist the team by being clear about the present state of knowledge of teachers in the school regarding crisis issues. Even students currently preparing to become teachers are getting minimal training in this area. Those who have been teaching for a long time, while they clearly have the important benefit of experience, rarely will have had academic training in crisis management.

Responsibility for this training has fallen mostly on school systems; therefore, a realistic representation of the need for training for teachers is essential to the crisis plan. All members of the crisis response team should undergo training. After they are trained themselves, teacher members of the crisis response team can assist in training other teachers in the school (see the section on professional development in chapter 9). All members of the crisis response team must be willing to devote the time that adequate training requires, and teachers considering the role should keep this in mind.

All members of the crisis response team will also have a role to play when a crisis occurs. The role of the crisis response team teacher during the crisis depends a great deal on the school's plan, the members of the team, and the strengths and experience of the individual teacher. Some roles that teachers who are members of the crisis response team are most likely to play include the following:

- communicator and role model for their own class
- communicator with other teachers
- manager of classes of students with special needs
- support to teachers whose class has experienced a crisis
- assistant in management of student records

When properly trained, teachers have every reason to feel as competent in their role as any other member of the team. This is important to remember, because the stress of a crisis can erode our confidence, especially when we are playing a role that is new to us.

THE CLASSROOM TEACHER NOT A MEMBER OF THE CRISIS RESPONSE TEAM

Not every teacher wants to be, should be, or can be a member of the crisis response team. Participation on the crisis response team should always be voluntary; however, every teacher must know about the team, know about the crisis intervention plan, and know how to access the services of the team when necessary.

Utilization of the services of the crisis response team is not an option but rather the obligation of every teacher. When the services should be accessed, that is, what is considered to be a crisis, while obvious in some circumstances, is not so clear in others. This issue should be discussed in teacher training by the crisis response team. Once agreed upon, the crisis response team procedures should be followed by the classroom teacher. Teachers who utilize the process but believe it was ineffective should make their feelings known when debriefings are carried out, that is, when the school's effectiveness in meeting the crisis is reviewed.

School crisis specialists have recommended that most crisis intervention assistance for students take place in the classroom (Brock et al., 2009; Poland, Pitcher, and Lazarus, 2002); therefore, teachers are key players in meeting the needs of their students. The effective crisis response team should be open to different methods of addressing needs and take the wishes and skills of the classroom teacher into account. The teacher who wishes to handle her class's crisis herself or who would like more than the amount of assistance usually offered should inform the crisis response team of her preference and explain her reasons; however, failure to involve the crisis response team at all can lead to difficulties if unexpected complications arise and can leave the teacher vulnerable to charges of negligence.

The school's crisis intervention plan should be readily available to the classroom teacher in two forms. The first should be a full description of the role of the teacher in a crisis in general, and any specific crisis in particular. That version should be reissued and read anew each year, since procedures will change. Read it and be sure you understand it. Ask questions if you do not, and do so early in the school year. Make reading the plan one of the things you do at the beginning of each school year.

The second form should be two quick and easy and perhaps tabbed books, pamphlets, or charts that briefly explain the procedures, codes, and recommendations. Each teacher should have this latter version handy. Yes, "It's 1 p.m., do you know where your crisis plan is?" would apply here. One copy should be kept in class, where it is also readily available to substitute and student teachers. The other should be kept in a secure location at home, since that is where you may be when you first hear of the occurrence of some crises.

Those experiencing trauma have a hierarchy of needs. Keeping these needs in mind will help the teacher know where to begin in helping students in crisis. School personnel must first be concerned with students' physical safety, then the worries and needs of students' family members, and third, the needs of all involved to have accurate information and reassurance (Yule, 2001).

THE TEACHER'S ROLE DURING AND AFTER A CRISIS

Organizer and Facilitator

When a crisis hits schools, whether it is as close as children shot on your playground or as distant as a plane hitting a building in another city, the teacher is usually the adult who is with America's youth at the time. He is the adult in charge. In many ways, both legal and practical, the school is the child's protector during a crisis, and the school's representative for any given child, the person on the scene, is that child's teacher. The more the teacher knows about what to do in crisis situations, the safer America's children will be, in terms of both their physical and their mental health. The following are some practical tips for the teacher during a crisis:

- Do not move or touch suspicious devices (they could be explosive) (Trump, 2002).
- Be sure all of your students are accounted for, and notify crisis managers immediately if they are not.
- Do not move or touch things in the classroom that could provide clues or other important information after the event.
- Follow crisis response team plans with regard to who talks to the media, who is stationed where, and when and how to communicate with parents.

If You Must Leave Your Room

Schools should have necessary crisis materials ready to go to a different site should that become necessary. These materials are sometimes called crisis response boxes or go-kits. A specific list of what should be in a go-kit can be found at http://rems.ed.gov. You should know what is in your school's crisis box, who will have it at the site (if that person is someone other than each classroom teacher), and how to access what your class needs from the box. As a teacher responsible for a class, you should take a minimum of the following items if you must leave your classroom:

- a complete list of students
- a list of parent names, addresses, and phone numbers
- your purse or attaché, whatever may contain important personal belongings like house and car keys, driver's license, or personal medications
- a small bag that acts as a carryall with a list of things you must take so that you will remember what is needed
- the brief version of the school crisis intervention plan
- some easy-to-carry materials so students will have something to occupy them at the location to which they are taken (Poland, 1994)

- anything else that might be helpful to a class of students that age that is not already in the school's crisis box

Communicator

Accurate information, communicated at the appropriate developmental level for the children in question, is important for crisis management and for the children's effective adjustment after the crisis event. Since teachers are used to communicating at a level appropriate to the grades they teach, they will have this skill already developed. The school's crisis plan should include a method for getting necessary information to classroom teachers, who should then communicate with their students. For events that do not present immediate risk to the students, teachers should wait until the information is confirmed before talking with the class.

In a review of how the events of 9/11 were handled in her school district, Dreshman (2002) suggests that schools have a communication room where television and radio can be monitored and that there be a designated communication person to visit classrooms to keep teachers accurately informed. Her experience showed that the use of television in the classroom during a crisis can disrupt the school day and lead to communication of inconsistent and confusing information that fosters emotional overreaction.

Since that time, research on that and other events has indicated that visual exposure to crisis events should be limited. There is evidence that this repeated exposure actually contributes to Post-Traumatic Stress Disorder in children. It brings the event close to those who would otherwise maintain some distance from it. Closeness to an event increases the risk of negative emotional reactions.

For events that do present a risk to the students, the school should have a communication system in place that is brief and clear. For example, if rooms are to be locked and shades drawn, a simple direction from the office should be sufficient, since school personnel will have been trained in advance in how to respond to the direction.

The first days that students return to school after a crisis event can be crucial in setting the tone for their adjustment. Different students are likely to require different approaches depending on their closeness to the event, their prior history, and their emotional makeup. The following are some general practical tips for teachers coming back to school after a crisis:

- Adjust classroom expectations and procedures appropriately. Maintenance of routine is helpful to students in a crisis; however, tests or presentations, often stressful in themselves, should be postponed if the class is relatively close to the event.
- Model effective problem solving.
- Model appropriate emotional expression. Reactions of caretakers have a significant effect on the reactions of children and youth. While it is appropriate to be sad and even tearful after an event, extremes of emotion in caretakers make it more difficult for children to cope.
- Provide accurate information. Rumor control is an appropriate function for the classroom teacher in any form of crisis. Rumors feed anxiety and tap energy needed for more constructive activities. Since so many members of the community come together in schools, the setting can be a breeding ground for rumor. It can also be a source of accurate and important information. Classroom teachers should take every opportunity to seek out accurate information for their students. They should also not simply dismiss inaccurate information passing among students, but address and correct it. If a piece of information could be true but has not been verified, that should also be shared with the students.
- Identify students in need of counseling and refer them to school mental health professionals without delay. Do not attempt to discuss a traumatic event with a child who has been directly involved. This process is delicate and should be left to a mental health professional.
- Observe student confidentiality, as appropriate. This issue involves all students, not just those directly involved. The media, for example, should not interview students without parent permission (Poland, Pitcher, and Lazarus, 2002).
- Be flexible with regard to involvement and communication with parents. It may be advisable, for example, for children to return to school with their parents the first day after a crisis event (Poland, Pitcher, and Lazarus, 2002).

- Write a brief but accurate report of what happened during the crisis. (Such a report may be of use to authorities, can assist in a legal investigation, and can be useful in crisis intervention debriefing.)
- Obtain necessary personal support for yourself. This is important, not only for the teacher's adjustment, but to his or her ability to assist students.

Because teachers often know about the families and friends of their students, they are in a unique position to assist mental health providers in locating students at most risk. For example, if a senior is killed in an automobile accident, teachers are most likely to know if he had siblings and what grades they are in. Teachers may also know who his best friends were. These other students in the school could be at high risk and should be mentioned to school psychologists and counselors for assessment of their needs in a crisis.

Teachers often wonder how much and what to say to the class after a crisis. Should you hold a discussion of the event? Should there be limits to that discussion? These are all excellent questions without easy answers; however, there are guidelines based on our experience of what has helped children and youth through past events. Your school crisis team should provide a written statement for the classroom teacher with verified information that can be shared with the class. It is important to stick to that information and not embellish what is provided with unverified rumor.

Students will have questions. Answer them honestly based on the information provided and say you don't know if you don't. Do not provide unnecessary or graphic detail regarding the incident. When possible, tie the information and the incident into teaching moments that help students see the value of reason and understanding in a crisis. Remember the following in holding your discussion:

- Students who have direct experience of the crisis, eye witnesses, for example, should not be part of class discussion with those who were not involved.
- Students who have extreme emotional reactions, perhaps due to emotional difficulties or past experiences, should not be part of the general classroom discussion.

- Discussions should be brief.
- You should talk about your plan for a discussion with a school mental health professional.
- You should not hold a discussion with your class if your own reaction to the event is intense.

Health Educator

In an article that makes a strong case for involving teachers in crisis intervention, Paris (1999) talks about the opportunity teachers have to educate students regarding appropriate ways to cope with crisis. She recommends that if students "share symptoms" of stress following a crisis, teachers inform students of the normalcy of their reactions.

Teachers can empower students by helping them brainstorm ways to cope and informing them of the importance of taking care of themselves by getting enough sleep, eating right, and exercising. Students should be asked to think about successful ways they have coped with stress in the past. Teachers can also help students prepare for anniversary dates of a crisis with discussion of possible reactions to anticipate and healthy ways to cope.

Special Services Provider

Most teachers will have students with disabilities included in their classes, and some teachers will have whole classes of students with special needs. In most instances, the suggestions for intervention provided in section II of this book apply to them, as well; however, there are some students for whom these interventions will have to be modified much as one would modify any classroom experience for a child who learns and expresses himself differently from his or her peers.

It is of the utmost importance that students with disabilities be included in the crisis plan, not only in the most obvious sense of keeping them from physical harm, but it is also crucial that thought be given to how they will be assisted in coping with the grief, anxiety, and change that can result from trauma. Teachers who are special educators should be involved in this planning process. They are most likely to be aware of ways that the plan can and should be modified for exceptional students. These teachers should also be an integral part of the plan if special arrangements are necessary, for example, the use of sign language or assistive equipment.

In some ways, children with known special needs may be in a better position to receive help in coping with trauma, because they are likely to already have providers in the community who can assist with their adjustment. Students with retardation or emotional disabilities, for example, may already have case managers or therapists.

The downside of this circumstance is that services provided to these students can be fragmented and redundant if coordination is not done carefully. The teachers of students with special needs should, with parent permission, help service providers coordinate support during and after a crisis event. Every effort should be made to see that service provided at school does not interfere with that provided in the community.

Adaptation of crisis prevention and intervention techniques will differ depending on the nature of the disability. Those with such developmental disabilities as retardation and autism will often have cognitive limitations that require simpler, repetitive explanations of events and directions. Those with developmental disabilities are also more likely to be sensitive to the changes in routine that come about during and right after a crisis event.

Preventative measures with this population should include visual aids illustrating procedures for exiting the building and regular practice of these procedures. For example, the teacher might have large orange dots on the walls that are to be followed during fire drills. After several opportunities to practice, students with cognitive limitations may no longer need to follow the guides.

Another preventative measure is for students to leave the building in pairs. The intent is not to make the student without the disability responsible for the disabled peer. The safety of all students is the teacher's responsibility. The point here is to make exiting the building easier for students who may have trouble remembering the exact route, especially when it is first practiced.

Special explanations of crisis events should be provided to students with cognitive disabilities. The teacher who spends the most time with the student is probably the best one to provide the explanation, because he is most likely to know the level of communication most appropriate.

Sometimes explanations are best given by resource teachers or other special educators, because they can see the students in smaller groups or one on one.

Students with physical disabilities present special challenges with regard to exiting the building in a timely fashion. This must be planned for in advance and should include arrangements to have all of the student's supports, medical and orthopedic, available in a central location that can be accessed wherever the student happens to be. Medications and medical supplies should be kept in a portable container, and the person responsible to bring them along, in the event that the building has to be vacated, should be identified in the crisis plan.

Those with hearing and vision problems need assistance mostly in the arena of communication. Again, advance identification of the staff person responsible for ensuring that the student leaves the building safely is essential. If the student signs, the responsible adult should be able to sign.

Students with emotional disabilities also require that a staff support person be identified in advance. Advance planning should include brainstorming about the potential reaction of the student with emotional problems, given the student's background and diagnosis. Depressed and anxious students, also known as those with internalizing disorders, are more likely to need therapeutic intervention after a school crisis than those whose disorders are manifested by conduct problems, assuming, of course, that the student with conduct problems was not directly involved and does not have other characteristics that would put him or her at risk.

Specifics on how crisis intervention issues will be addressed for students with disabilities should appear not only in the school's crisis plan, but also in the student's individual education plan. The writing of the individual education plan is another area in which the teacher should play a primary role.

Children whose first language is not English may also represent a population with special needs during a crisis. Ideally, someone who speaks their language should be available to those whose English is limited. This is not always possible in schools where large numbers of languages are represented. At the very least, someone should be designated to assist and support these students.

The language issue is also relevant in communication during or right after a crisis with families who are not English proficient. Plans for communication with these families during a crisis should be an integral part of the school crisis plan. It is the classroom teacher's role to remind team planners of the presence of a family who does not speak English. Each classroom teacher should know in advance how families who do not speak English will learn of school crises and how they will be given the suggestions for use at home that are provided to all families.

SUMMARY

In this chapter, we discussed the makeup and responsibilities of crisis response teams in the school. We discussed the role of teachers who are members of the team and those who work with the team to serve the students in their own classes. The teacher's role as organizer and facilitator, communicator, health educator, and special services provider was described. Fulfilling all of these roles takes training and practice. Teachers are in a unique position to inform school district planners of the training and resource needs of the buildings in which they work.

CHAPTER 12

The Teacher as Advocate

> Involvement of teachers is an important facet of creating successful prevention models. . . . It is the teacher who will have the greatest cumulative effect on the greatest number of students.
>
> —Lamden, King, and Goldman, 2002, p. 100

The number and type of in-school support services available to children varies widely depending on geographic location, financial status of the school system and its population, and cultural climate of the community. The opportunity the school has to access services in the surrounding community and the level of service there also varies.

Regardless of the services available, one of the most important ways for students to access them is through teacher referral. Even when parents are aware of a service they would like their child to receive, the person they are likely to discuss it with first is the classroom teacher. A teacher who does not know what support services his district can provide to children is like a family physician who does not know how to refer to specialists like neurologists or cardiologists. Such a physician would certainly be putting the health of her patients at risk.

WHAT THE TEACHER SHOULD KNOW ABOUT SUPPORT SERVICES

Professional Roles of Support Staff

To access appropriate services for students, it is essential that teachers know the roles of various support personnel available in schools.

Table 12.1.   School Support Personnel and Their Roles

Professional Title	Role
school psychologist	Mental health professional. Assesses social/emotional and educational needs of students. Provides child counseling, family interventions, consultation to teachers, and crisis intervention. Will usually have at least a master's degree plus an additional two years of training and may have a doctoral degree. All schools have access to this professional, although is it is rare for a school psychologist to have responsibility for just one school.
school counselor	Mental health professional. Provides affective education to classes, including whole-class and small groups, and counseling. Will usually have a bachelor's or master's degree. Most schools will have access to this professional. Counselors usually serve one school.
school social worker	Mental health professional. Most often responsible for family, court, and community agency contacts. Will usually have a master's degree. Not all schools offer this service. School social workers will often serve more than one school.
school nurse	Medical professional. Responsible for health and medication-related issues. Will usually have a bachelor's degree. Most schools will have access to this service. School nurses usually serve one or two schools, but sometimes more.

While the specifics of these roles may vary from system to system and even from school to school, training and basic responsibilities of most support personnel are common across systems. Table 12.1 contains a list of the most common support personnel in schools and their roles. Effective use of these services can assist the classroom teacher in crisis prevention and help lessen the negative impact of a crisis that does occur.

How to Refer

Every teacher knows that, even in the most affluent schools, student needs usually outpace available services. Given that reality, some process is necessary to determine where resources should be placed. These procedures are not always systematic and can be based on the "squeaky wheel" principle. Some kind of problem emerges, and then services are offered. By the time the services are provided, those involved are already frustrated and impatient to find a solution. There should be a better way, and there is. That way is for teachers to function as effective screeners and to flag students who need services the most. To do this well, teachers must effectively communicate student needs to those who offer services.

Sometimes the classroom teacher can get assistance by contacting the appropriate individual cited in table 12.1. In smaller schools, teachers may know these individuals personally and can talk to them about a child and get advice on a logical next step. If your school or district is small enough to allow for these personal contacts, that direct method can be very effective. Many teachers work in large districts where personal contact with support staff is difficult to maintain, or in rural districts where support personnel are stretched thin and travel long distances from school to school. In both instances, more formal procedures may be necessary for a teacher to make contact with support staff.

Teachers should become aware of the process for accessing these services as soon as they begin to teach at any school. The process may be different from school to school in the same district and may change from year to year even in the same school. The effective teacher should check on the procedure in place at the beginning of each school year.

Procedures for accessing support service for a child can range from simply filling out a one-page referral form to scheduling a formal meeting to discuss the child in question. (Crisis referrals should be handled differently and are discussed in the next section.) What the teacher is expected to do to address the problem prior to referral also varies, as will those attending the meeting. In general, however, to get the best result from a referral to support staff, the classroom teacher should do the following:

- Provide a specific description of the behavior or issue in question. How often does it occur? When did it appear?
- Provide a specific description of what has been done to address the problem. How often has it been tried? What was the result?
- Explain why the referral is being made at this time. Has the behavior worsened? Did the parent request the referral?
- Provide a brief review of the child's academic status. Grades? Achievement test scores? History? Work completion?

Having this information available in advance will help support personnel formulate relevant questions and learn what information might still need to be gathered. It is also best practice for the teacher to have made contact with the parent to discuss concerns. This will often lead to an explanation or at least additional information about whether the behavior at issue takes place at home or only at school. When resources are scarce, it is important to make the most efficient use of what is available. Teachers who come to meetings prepared make it easier for support teams to serve children in a timely fashion.

In some instances, the teacher cannot wait for a formal referral process. Some circumstances that require immediate attention are when the teacher suspects abuse or neglect, detects suicidal ideation, or anticipates acts of aggression. Procedures for a crisis referral will usually be a bit different depending on the issue at hand.

It cannot be stressed enough that the process for getting services for a child in crisis should be known well ahead of the time that it is needed. Because we all tend to be less effective under stressful conditions, it is best to have these procedures memorized. No one procedure will be in place in all schools, so it is not possible to outline a process here; however, some of the most common problems teachers face when attempting to make a crisis referral and suggested action are listed in table 12.2.

CHANGING THE SYSTEM:
SPEAKING UP ABOUT UNMET NEEDS

The more sensitive you are to your students and the more you know about crisis intervention and response to trauma, the more aware you will be of their need for services. Research suggests that our children and youth have many mental health requirements that go unaddressed. The aware teacher may be in the stressful situation of seeing what should be done and knowing that it will not be done, at least not to the degree that it should be. That is a pretty difficult place to be day after day.

Living with the resultant stress can lead to burnout and the best teachers leaving the field. Learning to do more to address the child's needs yourself is only part of the solution. Advocacy is another part. There is no one right way to advocate for change. The best way is the

Table 12.2. Overcoming Problems in Making a Crisis Referral

Problem	Solution
The process requires that the teacher contact the support worker directly, but the appropriate worker is not available or has not responded to the teacher's contact.	Contact the school principal, or, in her or his absence, another administrator, and inform them of the seriousness of the situation.
The student's parent has asked that the teacher not request support services.	Parent permission is not required for teachers to contact school support personnel. Support personnel should be informed of the parent's reluctance, but the teacher is still obligated to access support service in a crisis situation.
The student has asked that the teacher not request support services.	Student permission is not required for teachers to contact school support personnel. Support personnel should be informed of the student's reluctance, but the teacher is still obligated to contact them. At some point in the intervention, someone should explain to the child, in developmentally appropriate language, why it was necessary for the teacher to seek help for the child.
The school principal does not believe the circumstance warrants intervention.	This is a sensitive issue requiring careful consideration of the situation and the teacher's personal circumstances. In many states educators are legally responsible for reporting concerns about the safety of students. To have reason to suspect the potential for harm and not take action could leave the teacher legally and ethically liable. Talking to someone else, such as a school psychologist or counselor, might help sort things out.
Intervention takes place but the crisis recurs or support personnel decide no intervention is necessary and the crisis recurs.	Since support personnel do not know the child as well as the classroom teacher who sees him regularly, it may take them a while to fully understand the magnitude of the problem or develop an appropriate intervention. Contact them again.
Support personnel recommend that the parent access mental health services outside of school and assume that has been done, but the teacher finds out that the parents did not follow through.	Do not assume that because a recommendation has been made and not followed that nothing else can be done. Research shows that referrals to outside agencies often are not followed up on for a variety of reasons. Contact support personnel again.

one that makes you feel that you are making a difference while still maintaining your peace of mind.

Some educators feel that advocacy is best done away from their own school settings. You might donate to local mental health facilities, become a member of their boards, or mentor a child in the community. You might become politically active or join such advocacy groups as the Council for Exceptional Children or the Association for Children with Learning Disabilities. In that way, you are separating your advocacy work from your professional relationships.

Other educators want to work for change in the system that they know best and that affects them and the children they work with most, their own schools. Schools interested in creating positive climates will offer teachers different and important ways to participate in decision-making. If your school offers that opportunity, volunteer to participate on planning committees for curriculum, home-school relations, in-service days, or the new school playground. Seek opportunities to get the issues you think are important on the agenda.

For example, if you have developed an interest in the crisis prevention and intervention issue, check to see if the appropriate related topics have been built into the curriculum. Has the home-school relations committee considered how parents will be supported in the event of a school crisis? Has crisis intervention and prevention been included in the faculty in-service plan? Participation on these committees is especially important for a teacher new to a school because it gives the opportunity to learn how decisions are made and how the system responds to suggestions for change.

Attendance at school board meetings is another way to learn which issues are considered important to the system in which you work and what decision-making process is utilized. Knowledge of the process will help you develop realistic expectations and goals, an important factor in avoidance of frustration and burnout.

Participation on the child study or instructional support teams described in chapter 9 enhances your professional development in several ways. First, you learn techniques from other members that help you address needs in your own classroom. Research shows that interventions in schools are more effective when teachers model them for other teachers. Second, you can have an impact on students throughout the school by making your own suggestions for how they might be best served. Trends noticed in these meetings, if bullying issues come up frequently, for example, can lead to schoolwide interventions that enhance school climate and reduce the likelihood of crisis events. These teams also provide the teacher members with access to administrators. You should take advantage of this opportunity to describe the needs you see at the school.

Finally, there is no substitute for being knowledgeable and aware. Education is a profession directly affected by law and politics. Find a way to stay abreast of developments in your field both in terms of best practice and political events. Belong to at least one professional organization, for example, Kappa Delta Pi, the National Education Association, the Council for Exceptional Children, the National Association for Gifted Children, or the National Science Teachers Association. (See appendix B for a more extensive list.) Most memberships include journals. Read the articles, and develop a professional reading plan for yourself in an area of education that interests you most.

Teachers can be a force for change. Do not assume that someone else must have already noticed a problem or that new teachers cannot have an impact. Stay with an issue if you believe it is important, and do not underestimate the value of your contribution.

SUMMARY

In this chapter, we discussed the teacher's role in bringing about change in the schools in which they work. Knowledge of and participation in the life of the school is important, as is staying aware of the latest developments in best practices in education and political developments affecting schools. With focused efforts, teachers can bring about systemic change.

Additional Reading

Canter, A. S., and S. A. Carroll. (1999). *Crisis Prevention and Response: A Collection of NASP Resources.* Bethesda, MD: National Association of School Psychologists.

Espelage, D. L., and S. M. Swearer (Eds.). (2004). *Bullying in American Schools.* Mahwah, NJ: Lawrence Erlbaum.

Feinberg, T., and N. Robey. (2008). Cyberbullying. *Principal Leadership*, 9, 10–14.

Garbarino, J., and deLara, E. (2002). *And Words Can Hurt Forever.* New York: Simon & Schuster.

Heath, M. A., and B. Dean. (2008). Preparing for an Earthquake: Information for Families and Schools. *Communique*, *37*(3), 1, 10–13.

Heath, M.A., and D. Sheen. (2005). *School-Based Crisis Intervention: Preparing All School Personnel to Assist.* New York: Guilford.

Mason, K. L. (2008). Cyberbullying: A Preliminary Assessment for School Personnel. *Psychology in the Schools*, *45*(4), 323–47.

Packard Foundation (2002). Children, Youth, and Gun Violence. *The Future of Children*, *12*(2), 316–34.

Pipher, M. (1994). *Reviving Ophelia: Saving the Selves of Adolescent Girls.* New York: G. P. Putnam and Sons.

Rando, T. A. (1991). *How to Go on Living When Someone You Love Dies.* New York: Putnam.

Sharlin, S. A., and A. Shenhar. (1986). The Fusion of Pressing Situation and Releasing Writing: On Adolescent Suicide Poetry. *Suicide and Life Threatening Behavior*, *16*(3), 343–55.

Swearer, S. M., L. Espelage, and S. A. Napolitano. (2009). *Bullying Prevention and Intervention: Realistic Strategies for Schools.* New York: Guilford.

Wolfelt, A. (1983). *Helping Children Cope with Grief.* Muncie, IN: Accelerated Development.

The following publications are about assisting children with disabilities in coping with crisis and loss:

Kasari, C., S. F. N. Freeman, and W. Bass. (2003). Empathy and Responses to Distress in Children with Down Syndrome. *Journal of Child Psychology and Psychiatry, 3443*(3), 424–31.
Lavin, C. (1998). Helping Individuals with Developmental Disabilities. In K. Doka and J. Davidson (Eds.), *Living with Grief: Who We Are, How We Grieve* (pp. 161–80). New York: Brunner and Rutledge.
National Association of School Psychologists. (2002). *Coping with Crisis— Helping Children with Special Needs: Tips for School Personnel and Parents.* Retrieved from www.nasponline.org/resources/crisis_safety/specpop_general.aspx.
Yanok, J., and J. A. Beifus. (1993). Communicating about Loss and Mourning: Death Education for Individuals with MR. *Mental Retardation, 3*(3), 144–47.

The following readings are for children and youth. Read all materials carefully in advance to be sure the perspective taken in the book is appropriate for the children in question and your educational environment. Plan ahead for questions you will ask and might get and how you will use the reading constructively.

Aboff, M., and K. Gartner. (2003). *Uncle Willy's Tickles: A Child's Right to Say No.* Washington, DC: American Psychological Association.
Cohn, J. (1994). *Why Did It Happen? Helping Children Cope in a Violent World.* New York: Morrow Junior Books.
Gootman, M. E. (1994). *When a Friend Dies: A Book for Teens about Grieving and Healing.* Minneapolis: Free Spirit Publishing.
Greenlee, S. (1992). *When Someone Dies.* Atlanta, GA: Peachtree Publishing.
Heegaard, M. E. (1992). *When Something Terrible Happens: Children Learn to Cope with Grief.* Minneapolis, MN: Woodland Press.
Holden, D. (2001). *Gran-Gran's Best Trick: A Story for Children Who Have Lost Someone They Love.* Washington, DC: American Psychological Association.

Holmes, M. M., and S. J. Mudlaff. (1999). *A Terrible Thing Happened.* Washington, DC: American Psychological Association.

Huebner, D. (2007). *What to Do When Your Temper Flares.* Weaverville, CA: Boulden.

Julik, E. (2000). *Sailing through the Storm: To the Ocean of Peace.* Valencia, PA: Glade Press.

Mark, B., and M. Chesworth. (1999). *I Know What I'll Do: A Kid's Guide to Natural Disasters.* Washington, DC: American Psychological Association.

Mills, J. (2003). *Gentle Willow: A Story for Children about Dying.* Washington, DC: American Psychological Association.

Mosher, A. (1994). *Don't Rant and Rave on Wednesdays!: The Children's Anger Control Book.* Kansas City, MO: Landmark Editions.

Pelligrino, M. (1998). *I Don't Have an Uncle Phil Anymore.* Washington, DC: American Psychological Association.

Peterkin, A. (1992). *What about Me?: When Brothers and Sisters Get Sick.* Washington, DC: American Psychological Association.

Rogers, F. (1998). *When a Pet Dies.* New York: Putnam Juvenile.

Sheppard, C. (1998). *Brave Bart: A Story for Traumatized and Grieving Children.* Grosse Pointe Woods, MI: National Institute for Trauma and Loss in Children.

Shuman, C. (2003). *Jenny Is Scared!: When Sad Things Happen in the World.* Washington, DC: American Psychological Association.

Wolfelt, A. (2001). *Healing Your Grieving Heart for Kids.* Ft. Collins, CO: Companion.

Organizations, Websites, and Materials

The World Wide Web is a great equalizer. In the context of crisis intervention and prevention, that means the classroom teacher, school principal, parent, and psychiatrist in the community have easy access to much of the same information. What a wonderful thing! However, it can also be a bit overwhelming. The sites listed in this appendix contain information likely to be of interest to the classroom teacher, but they also contain a lot of text that is extraneous to that role. It is suggested that you use these sites in the following ways:

- Narrow your focus by deciding what interests you most in this book and search according to those topics.
- Search the topics on crises that you are most likely to face before the crisis occurs. Even the most organized sites can be difficult to navigate under stress.
- Bookmark the sites that are most relevant to your situation.

ORGANIZATIONS

American Association of Suicidology
5221 Wisconsin Avenue NW
Washington, DC 20015
202-237-2280
www.suicidology.org

Brady Center to Prevent Handgun Violence
1225 Eye Street, Suite 1100
Washington, DC 20005
202-289-7319
www.bradycenter.org

Centers for Disease Control and Prevention
1600 Clifton Road
Atlanta, GA 30333
800-232-4636
www.cdc.gov

Council for Exceptional Children
110 North Glebe Road, Suite 300
Arlington, VA 22201
888-232-7733
www.cec.sped.org

Council for Learning Disabilities
11184 Antioch Road
PO Box 405
Overland Park, KS 66201
913-491-1011
www.cldinternational.org

Crisis Prevention Institute
10850 W Park Place, Suite 600
Milwaukee, WI 53224
800-558-8976
www.crisisprevention.com

The Good Grief Program of the Boston Medical Center Department of
    Pediatrics
Vose Hall, 403
92 East Concord Street
Boston, MA 02118
617-414-4005
www.bmc.org/pediatrics-goodgrief.htm

Military Child Initiative
615 North Wolf Street, E4527
Baltimore, MD 21205
www.jhsph.edu/mci
The purpose of this organization is to help schools address the needs of children in military families. It assists schools with assessing their capabilities in this area, outlines best practices, and offers resources to educators.

National Association for Beginning Teachers
2505 Anthem Village Drive, Suite 301
Henderson, NV 89052
888-246-0189
www.beginningteachers.org

National Association for Bilingual Education
1313 L Street, Suite 210
Washington, DC 20005-4100
202-898-1829
www.nabe.org

National Association for the Education of Young Children
1313 L Street NW, Suite 500
Washington, DC 20005
800-424-2460
www.naeyc.org/default/contact

National Association for Gifted Children
1707 L Street NW, Suite 550
Washington, DC 20036
202-785-4268
www.nagc.org

National Association of School Psychologists
4340 East West Highway, Suite 402
Bethesda, MD 20814
866-657-0270
www.nasponline.org

This organization quickly posts recommendations for schools following a national crisis event, sometimes within hours. Their suggestions are well-researched, timely, and intended specifically for educational settings. If you go to only one website following a crisis, this should be the one. You will also find excellent and extensive material on prevention in both the academic and mental health arenas.

National Center for Children Exposed to Violence
Yale University Child Study Center
230 South Frontage Road
New Haven, CT 06520-7900
877-49N-CCEV
www.nccev.org

National Center for Death Education
Mount Ida College
777 Dedham Street
Newton, MA 02459
617-928-4649
www.mountida.edu/sp.cfm?pageid=307

National Council for History Education
7100 Baltimore Avenue, Suite 510
College Park, MD 20740
440-835-1776
www.nche.net

National Council for the Social Studies
8555 Sixteenth Street
Silver Spring, MD 20910
301-588-1800
www.socialstudies.org

National Council of Teachers of English
1111 W Kenyon Road
Urbana, IL 61801-1096
877-369-6283
www.ncte.org

National Council of Teachers of Mathematics
1906 Association Drive
Reston, VA 20190-1502
800-235-7566
www.nctm.org

National Education Association
1201 16th Street NW
Washington, DC 20036
202-833-4000
www.nea.org
www.neahin.org/crisis/guide
HIN in the title stands for Health Information Network. This National
Education Association website includes an extensive crisis guide that
addresses crisis topics that arise before, during, and after a crisis.

National Organization for Victim Assistance
510 King Street, Suite 424
Alexandria, VA 22314
703-735-NOVA
www.trynova.org
This site offers formal training in crisis intervention.

National Science Teachers Association
1840 Wilson Boulevard
Arlington, VA 22201
703-243-7100
www.nsta.org

SafetyLit
6505 Alvarado Road, Suite 105
San Diego, CA 92120
619-594-1994
www.safetylit.org
This organization provides abstracts of research literature on health and
safety issues. It is a service of the San Diego State University School
of Public Health and the World Health Organization.

SPAN (Suicide Prevention Action Network) USA, Inc.
1010 Vermont Avenue NW, Suite 408
Washington, DC 20005
202-449-3600
www.spanUSA.org

U.S. Department of Education Safe and Drug Free Schools Program
550 12th Street SW, 10th Floor
Washington, DC 20202-6450
202-245-7896
www2.ed.gov/aboutoffices/list/osdfs/contacts.html

WEBSITES

Centers for Disease Control and Prevention Effective School Programs
www.cdc.gov/HealthyYouth/index.htm

Centers for Disease Control and Prevention Federal and State List of
Suicide Legislation
www2a.cdc.gov/phlp/suicide legislation.asp

Centers for Disease Control and Prevention National Advisory Committee on Children and Terrorism
www.bt.cdc.gov/children/index.asp
From this site, you can download A *Center Quick Training Aid: School-Based Crisis Intervention* (2002), which includes topics, handouts, and exercises for use in training school teams in crisis prevention and intervention, as well as a long list of relevant publications and websites. Also available are *A Center Training Tutorial: Crisis Assistance and Prevention: Reducing Barriers to Learning* (2004) and *Responding to Crisis at a School* (2005). These publications include information related to different crises educators are likely to face and specific recommendations for intervention, with readings and overheads to aid in training.

Cyberbullying Research Center
www.cyberbullying.us

This website contains a full range of information on recognizing and intervening in cyberbullying, as well as a review of current laws and prevention measures.

Federal Emergency Management Agency for Kids
www.fema.gov/kids/

Federal Emergency Management Institute
www.training.fema.gov/emiweb/is/
This site offers training for educators on the National Incident Management System.

Military Students on the Move: A Toolkit for Military Parents
www.k12.wa.US/OperationMilitaryKids/pubdocs/ParentsToolkit_0406.pdf

National Association of School Psychologists
www.nasponline.org/families/index/aspx
Information on this website is for families and offers a wide range of topics for exploration by educators assisting families and the families themselves.

National Association of School Psychologists PREPaRE School Crisis
    Prevention and Intervention Training Curriculum
www.nasponline.org/prepare/index/aspx
This website provides an introduction and information on training in PREPaRE, the school crisis prevention and intervention training program devised for educators by the National Association of School Psychologists. Trainees do not have to be school psychologists to participate. All educators are welcome.

National Child Traumatic Stress Network Military Families Knowl-
    edge Bank
www.nctsnet.org

National Register of Evidence-Based Programs and Practices
1-866-43N-REPP

www.nrepp.samhsa.gov/
This website helps schools in meeting the legal requirement to use da-tabased interventions in schools.

National Youth Violence Prevention Resource Center
www.safeyouth.org/scripts/index.asp
This site is a good source of information about youth violence and suicide prevention.

The Ophelia Project
www.opheliaproject.org
This site focuses on signs of and interventions for relational aggression.

Paperbacks for Educators
www.any-book-in-print.com/
This website offers titles related to bibliotherapy.

Positive Behavioral Supports
www.pbis.org

Readiness and Emergency Management for Schools Technical Assistance Center
http://rems.ed.gov
This is the federal School Emergency Management website. If you are interested in a site with a full background on emergency procedures and policies, this is the one. It offers extensive resources for writing school emergency policies, planning for drills and go-kits, and devel-oping forms. Training and grant opportunities are provided.

Suicide Prevention Resource Center
www.sprc.org

UCLA School Mental Health Project Center for Mental Health in Schools
PO Box 951563
Los Angeles, CA 90095-1563

866-846-4843
http://smhp.psych.ucla.edu/

MATERIALS

Break It Up: A Teacher's Guide for Managing Student Aggression
  (1995)
By A. Goldstein, J. Palumbo, S. Striepling, and A. Vautsinas
Book and video available through Research Press
www.researchpress.com

*Bully Busters: A Teacher's Manual for Helping Bullies, Victims, and
Bystanders (Grades K–5)* (2003)
By A. M. Horne, C. L. Bartolomucci, and D. Newman-Carlson
Available through Research Press
www.researchpress.com

The Good Behavior Game
The PAX Good Behavior Game Schoolwide Implementation Guide
  (2003)
By D. Embry, G. Straatemeier, K. Lauger, and C. Richardson
Published by Hazeldon Publishers
info@hazeldon.org

Olweus Bullying Prevention Program Training Manual (2003)
By D. Olweus, S. P. Limber, N. Mullin-Rindler, N. Riese, V. Flerx,
and M. Snyder
Available through Clemson University
www.clemson.edu/olweus/

The PATHS Curriculum (1994)
By C. A. Kusche and M. T. Greenberg
Developmental Research Programs
Seattle, WA
www.channingbete.com

Second Step: A Violence Prevention Program
By K. Beland and T. White
2203 Airport Way South, Suite 500
Seattle, Washington 98134
Available from the Committee for Children
www.cfchildren.org

Thanks to Amy Matz at the Indiana University of Pennsylvania Child
Study Center for her assistance in compiling this list.

Important Terms

affect: A psychological and medical term meaning emotion. Affective education involves helping children learn about emotions and behavior and how to cope effectively. The term is pronounced ah'fect, not eefect'.

antidepressants: Medications prescribed for depression. There are several different types. They may be identified by their chemical names or by brand names. Zoloft, for example, is the brand name for the antidepressant sertraline. Paxil is the brand name for paroxetine. These medications will most often be identified by their brand names. All must be prescribed by a medical professional. It is outside the teacher's field of expertise to recommend medications.

behaviorism: A theoretical construct that emphasizes the importance of learning, reward, and consequences in the development of behavior patterns in adults and children.

Bipolar Disorder: An illness affecting mood where individuals experience periods of depression alternating with periods of mostly normal mood or periods of depression and excessive elation. *Common area of confusion:* Bipolar disorder used to be known as manic depressive illness. The latter term is no longer used.

certification: A term typically used to identify professionals who have met qualifications to practice their profession in the schools. The gatekeeper of this credential is the state in which the school is located. Counselors, social workers, and psychologists usually have to be certified to work in schools, even if they are licensed to private practice in the community. *Common area of confusion:* A license usually means credentialed to practice privately, and certification means credentialed to work in schools; however, in some states the term license is also used for the school credential. Teachers should know which term is used in their state.

clinical psychologist: A mental health professional with at least a master's degree, but usually a doctorate. Most licensed psychologists doing outpatient therapy in private practices are clinical psychologists. *Common area of confusion:* Psychologists cannot prescribe medications and should not be confused with psychiatrists who are medical doctors with a specialty in psychiatry. Many licensed psychologists do, however, have hospital privileges, that is, they can make arrangements for psychiatric inpatient treatment, if necessary.

cognitive intervention: A form of counseling assistance that helps the client think differently about a problem. Procedures that teach a child steps to follow in solving a problem, that help a child think before engaging in a behavior, or that help a student visualize herself doing a particular thing are all examples of cognitive interventions. These procedures can be used successfully in such academic interventions as teaching methods to improve attention and memory or in behavior management programs where children brainstorm ways a problematic situation might be handled.

counseling: A professional helping relationship between a mental health practitioner and a client typically seeking short-term help with problems in living. This term is often used interchangeably with therapy or psychotherapy; however, the term *therapy* is sometimes reserved for longer-term treatment addressing a diagnosed mental health problem.

counselor: This term has several different meanings. When used in a general way, it can mean anyone who does mental health counseling, for example, a psychologist, social worker, or pastor. It can also be used to identify those certified to work in schools (sometimes called school counselors or guidance counselors) who teach affective education; do short-term counseling for school-related problems; and assist in course, vocational, and college planning. In some states counselors are licensed professionals in private practice who address a wide range of mental health problems. *Common area of confusion:*

School counselors are different from school psychologists. Counselors may work in schools with a master's and sometimes even a bachelor's degree. School psychologists have at least three years of graduate education. Psychologists are more often involved in identification of student disability and crisis intervention, although the roles of both professionals may vary depending on the procedures in any one school.

critical incident stress debriefing (CISD): A discussion of the event by those who have experienced a traumatic incident (usually in a group, but it can be done individually) and their reactions to it. The meeting is usually facilitated by a mental health professional experienced in the intervention. There is some question about whether these meetings are effective and how soon after the event they should take place.

critical incident stress management (CISM): The larger process of assisting those who have experienced a trauma. It includes planning for crises and interventions and reviews of how the incidents were managed.

cyberbullying: Intimidation of one individual by another involving threats of physical, emotional, or social status harm that is carried out through such electronic means as texting, e-mail, or online social sites.

depression: The medical and psychological term for a condition characterized by some combination of sadness, anger, lack of motivation, or lethargy experienced for a period of six months or more. Depression in children and adolescents may be different from that of adults; therefore, depression in this younger group can go unrecognized by educators. Research suggests that depression in any population may be the result of chemical imbalance combined with life stressors. Medication can be prescribed for this condition, even for children; however, the effects of medication with this population are less well-known than effects for adults, and there are indications that some medications may put young people at risk. Depression is not an educational term; however, under federal special education law, significant depression may be classified as emotional disturbance. Diagnoses of depression should be made by a mental health professional.

eating disorder: Sometimes identified more specifically as anorexia or bulimia. Eating disorders are characterized by a variety of maladaptive eating patterns, including minimal intake, bingeing, purging, or repetitive and excessive use of a narrow group of foods. The disorder is most often seen in teen and preteen girls. Eating disorders can be life threatening and warrant referral to a mental health professional.

encopresis: A medical term for inability to control bowel function. The condition may have a physiological or psychological cause.

enuresis: A medical term for inability to control bladder function. The condition may have a physiological or psychological cause.

externalized disorder: A psychological term for problems that show themselves by the child's acting out on the environment. Aggression and noncompliance are some characteristics of externalized disorders.

guidance counselor. *See* school counselor.

internalized disorder: A psychological term for problems that show themselves by effect on the child. Anxiety and such somatic symptoms as gastrointestinal problems and headaches are some characteristics of internalized disorders.

license: A term typically used to identify professionals who have met qualifications to practice their profession privately in the community. Gatekeepers for this credential are usually the state in which the practice is located and a board made up of professionals in the field. *Common area of confusion:* In some states, this term is used for a school credential. *See also* certification.

neurotic: The experience of neurosis. This is an outdated term and is no longer found in descriptions of those with mental health problems.

National Incident Management System (NIMS): Primarily an organizational and coordination system for the management of crisis situations among federal, state, and local agencies. Those complying with NIMS requirements receive training and institute an Incident Command System that identifies the roles and responsibilities at different levels of the management system.

Post-Traumatic Stress Disorder (PTSD): A medical and psychological term used to identify a disorder that sometimes develops in those who have experienced a traumatic event. Symptoms include sleep disturbance, anxiety, flashbacks, difficulty with concentration, and depression, but not all of these factors must be present for a diagnosis of PTSD. The disorder can be present in those of any age. It is believed that appropriate crisis management can lessen the likelihood of PTSD in crisis victims, but there are many other variables that contribute to whether the disorder will emerge in any one individual.

psychiatrist: A medical professional with at least four years of medical school after the bachelor's degree and several years of training beyond that to specialize in psychiatry (even more if they are pediatric psychiatrists, that is, trained specifically to work with children). Psychiatrists are rarely employed by schools, unless state special education regulations require their involvement in determination of special service eligibility for children with emotional disturbance. *Common areas of confusion:* Psychologists and psychiatrists are not the same profession, although both may go by the title of doctor. Psychologists have graduate degrees in psychology and have not attended medical school. Psychiatrists may prescribe medications for emotional and behavioral disorders, while psychologists may not.

psychologist: A general term used to describe anyone with a doctoral degree in psychology. Psychologists may specialize in many different areas, including industrial, social, neurological, or geriatric fields, among others. Psychologists most likely to serve school-age children are school, clinical, or pediatric psychologists. (School psychologists may have three years of graduate training or a doctorate.) To work in public schools, school psychologists must have an additional credential usually called a certification. *Common area of confusion:* Psychologists and psychiatrists are not the same professional. Psychiatrists have medical degrees, that is, they become physicians first and then specialize in psychiatry.

psychotic: A medical and psychological term used to describe a state of mind in which the individual has broken with reality. Psychotic individuals may hear voices and believe they are someone else or somewhere else. The term suggests the presence of serious mental illness, although medications can be quite effective in improving the quality of life for those with this disorder. *Common areas of confusion:* The common use of the term *psychotic killer* represents a misunderstanding of this word. Those who commit crimes, whether or not they may have other forms of mental illness, are not usually psychotic. Psychosis is rare among children and rare in general; however, when it does occur, adolescence is often the time of onset.

relational aggression: A form of bullying where intimidation of one individual by another is based on threats to harm or destroy the friendships or other relationships of the victim. It is more common among girls than boys.

resilience: A psychological term meaning ability to live a healthy productive life in spite of having experienced significant trauma. Certain characteristics in the individual and in environments are said to foster resilience. Learning about resilient individuals helps mental health professionals foster these characteristics in the children with whom they work.

school counselor: A certified education and mental health professional with training in counseling, vocational guidance, and affective education. Counselors working with children in elementary school often focus on mental health issues. Those working at the secondary level often focus more on college selection/application and scheduling. School counselors may have bachelor's or master's degrees and rarely have doctorates.

school psychologist: A certified education and mental health professional with usually at least three years of graduate training after the bachelor's degree who has studied child development, diagnosis of learning disorders, educational consultation, behavior management, counseling, and theories of learning. It is not uncommon for school psychologists to have doctoral degrees. Most school psychologists work in schools with children in grades K–12; however, some are employed in other settings. *Common areas of confusion:* School counselors and school psychologists are not the same professional. Counselors are more likely to do affective education for the general population in schools. They are less likely to be central players in diagnosis for special education services.

school social worker: A mental health professional sometimes employed by schools who usually has a master's degree. Sometimes those with a bachelor's degree will be identified by this term, but that is really an inappropriate use of the title. The role of the school social worker is usually to work with families of students who have difficulties. On school assessment teams, they are most likely to be the ones to take a family history. They also are often involved in truancy cases and facilitate school communication with other community systems, for example, mental health and justice. In the mental health community it is not uncommon for social workers to do counseling and crisis intervention. This is less likely in schools, but social workers do occasionally play this role.

References

Aberson, B., and M. Shure. (2002). Problem-Solving Training as a Form of Crisis Prevention. In S. Brock, P. Lazarus, and S. Jimerson (Eds.), *Best Practices in School Crisis Prevention and Intervention* (pp. 109–30). Bethesda, MD: National Association of School Psychologists.

Able, D. (2004, May 5). Donations Flowing again for Columbine Memorial. *Rocky Mountain News*. Retrieved from www.rockymountainnews.com/drmn/columbine/article/0,1299,DRMN_106_28642,00.html.

Aguilera, D. C. (1998). *Crisis Intervention: Theory and Methodology*. St. Louis: Mosby.

Allen, M., B. Y. Asbaker, and K. A. Scott. (2003). *Strengthening Rural Schools: Training Paraprofessionals in Crisis Prevention and Intervention*. In Proceedings of the American Council on Rural Special Education, Salt Lake City, UT (ERIC Document Reproduction Service No. ED476220).

American Association of Suicidology. (2010). Some Facts about Suicide in the U.S.A. Retrieved from www.suicidology.org.

American Psychiatric Association. (2000). *Diagnostic and Statistical Manual of Mental Disorders* (4th ed.). Washington, DC: Author.

American Red Cross of the Greater Lehigh Valley. (2010). *Disaster Services*. Retrieved from www.redcrosslv.org/disaster/disasterclass.html.

Aseltine, R. H. (2003). An Evaluation of a School-Based Suicide Prevention Program. *Adolescent and Family Health*, *3*(2), 81–88.

Aseltine, R. H., and R. DeMartino. (2004). An Outcome Evaluation of the SOS Suicide Prevention Program. *American Journal of Public Health*, *94*(3), 446–51.

Aseltine, R. H., A. James, E. A. Schilling, and J. Glanovsky. (2007). Evaluating the SOS Suicide Prevention Program: A Replication and Extension. Retrieved from www.biomedcentral.com/1471-2458/7/161.

Barnard, J. (1998, May 22). School Shooting Suspect Arraigned. *The Indiana Gazette*, p. 10.

Bear, G. G., A. R. Cavalier, and M. A. Manning. (2002). Best Practices in School Discipline. In A. Thomas and J. Grimes (Eds.), *Best Practices in School Psychology IV* (pp. 977–91). Bethesda, MD: National Association of School Psychologists.

Becker, G. (1998, April 27). More Student Violence Likely Unless Schools, Parents Act. *Indiana Gazette*, p. 3.

Berkowitz, S. J. (2003). Children Exposed to Community Violence: The Rationale for Early Intervention. *Clinical Child and Family Psychology Review*, 6(4), 293–302.

Blank, J., J. Vest, and S. Parker. (1998, April 6). The Children of Jonesboro. *U.S. News and World Report*, 124(13), 16–22.

Blom, G. E., B. D. Cheney, and J. E. Snoddy. (1986). *Stress in Childhood: An Intervention Model for Teachers and Other Professionals*. New York: Teachers College Press.

Bowman, B. T. (1994). Home and School: The Unresolved Relationship. In S. L. Kagan and B. Weissbourd (Eds.), *Putting Families First* (pp. 51–72). San Francisco: Jossey-Bass.

Bradshaw, C. P., M. Sudhinaraset, K. Mmari, and R. W. Blum. (2010). School Transitions among Military Adolescents: A Qualitative Study of Stress and Coping. *School Psychology Review*, 39(1), 84–105.

Brewin, C. R. (2001). Cognitive and Emotional Reactions to Traumatic Events: Implications for Short-Term Intervention [Electronic Version]. *Advances in Mind-Body Medicine*, 17(3), 163–69.

Brock, S. (2002). School Suicide Postvention. In S. Brock, P. Lazarus, and S. Jimerson (Eds.), *Best Practices in School Crisis Prevention and Intervention* (pp. 553–76). Bethesda, MD: National Association of School Psychologists.

Brock, S. E., A. B. Nickerson, M. A. Reeves, S. R. Jimerson, R. A. Lieberman, and T. A. Feinberg. (2009). *School Crisis Prevention and Intervention: The PREPaRE Model*. Bethesda, MD: National Association of School Psychologists.

Brock, S. E., J. Sandoval, and S. Lewis. (2001). *Preparing for Crises in the Schools: A Manual for Building School Crisis Response Teams* (2nd ed.). New York: Wiley.

Brooks, B., and P. M. Siegel. (1996). *The Scared Child*. New York: John Wiley.

Brooks, R. B. (2002). Creating Nurturing Classroom Environments: Fostering Hope and Resilience as an Antidote to Violence. In S. Brock, P. Lazarus, and S. Jimerson (Eds.), *Best Practices in School Crisis Prevention and*

Intervention (pp. 67–93). Bethesda, MD: National Association of School Psychologists.

Burns, M. K., V. J. Dean, and S. Jacob-Timm. (2001). Assessment of Violence Potential among School Children: Beyond Profiling. *Psychology in the Schools, 38*(3), 239–47.

Callahan, C. J. (1998). Crisis Intervention Model for Teachers [Electronic Version]. *Journal of Instructional Psychology, 25*(4), 226–35.

Carroll, S. (1997). Emotional First Aid: A School's Guide to Crisis Intervention. *Communique, 11*(5), 17–37.

CBSNews.com. (2003, April 24). PA Principal Killed by Eighth-Grader. Retrieved from www.cbsnews.com/stories/2003/04/25/national/main551088 .shtml.

Christenson, S. L., and S. M. Sheridan. (2001). *Schools and Families.* New York: Guilford.

CNN. (1998, June 11). Woodham Testifies He Was Involved in Satanism. Retrieved from www.cnn.com/us/9806/11/schoolshooting.03/#top.

CNN.com. (2005, March 22). School Gunman Stole Police Pistol, Vest. Retrieved from www.cnn.com/2005/US/03/22/school.shooting/index.html.

Crisis Prevention Institute. (1994). *Nonviolent Crisis Intervention for the Educator: Fights at School.* Brookfield, WI: Author.

Crisis Prevention Institute. (2005). *Nonviolent Crisis Intervention Training Program.* Brookfield, WI: Author.

Crisis Prevention Institute. (2010). About CPI. Retrieved from www.crisis prevention.com/About-CPI.

Cronin, M. E., D. L. Slade, C. Bechtel, and P. Anderson. (1992). Home-School Partnerships: A Cooperative Approach to Intervention. *Intervention in School and Clinic, 27*(5), 286–92.

Cullen, D. (2009). *Columbine.* New York: Twelve.

Dattilio, F. M., and A. Freeman. (2000). *Cognitive-Behavioral Strategies in Crisis Intervention.* New York: Guilford.

DeFlitch, G. (1997, December 21). Officials, Teachers on Front Line to Spot Troubled Teenagers. *Indiana Gazette,* pp. A1, A14.

Dinkmeyer, D. (1970, 1982). *Developing Understanding of Self and Others.* Circle Pines, MN: American Guidance Service.

Doll, B., and J. A. Cummings. (2008). *Transforming School Mental Health Services.* Thousand Oaks, CA: Corwin; Bethesda, MD: National Association of School Psychologists.

Doll, B., and M. A. Lyon. (1998). Risk and Resilience: Implications for the Delivery of Educational and Mental Health Services in Schools. *School Psychology Review, 27*(3), 348–63.

Dorwart, R. A., and M. J. Ostacher. (1999). A Community Psychiatry Approach to Preventing Suicide. In D. G. Jacobs (Ed.), *Guide to Suicide Assessment and Intervention* (pp. 52–71). San Francisco: Jossey-Bass.

Dreshman, J. (2002). Crisis Response and 9-11: What We Have Learned. *PA CASSP Newsletter, 11*(1), 3–4.

Dwyer, K. (1998). Children Killing Children: Strategies to Prevent Youth Violence. *Communique, 27*(3), 1, 9.

Egan, T. (1998, May 22). Oregon Student Held in 3 Killings: One Dead, 23 Hurt at His School. *New York Times*, p. A20.

Embry, D. D. (2002). The Good Behavior Game: A Best Practice Candidate as a Universal Behavioral Vaccine [Electronic Version]. *Clinical Child and Family Psychology Review, 5*(4), 273–97.

Emery, R. E., and R. Forehand. (1994). Parental Divorce and Children's Well-Being: A Focus on Resilience. In R. J. Haggerty, L. R. Sherrod, N. Garmezy, and M. Rutter (Eds.), *Stress, Risk, and Resilience in Children and Adolescents* (pp. 64–99). Cambridge, UK: Cambridge University Press.

Espelage, D. L., and S. M. Swearer. (2008). Addressing Research Gaps in the Intersection between Homophobia and Bullying. *School Psychology Review, 37*(2), 155–59.

Farmer, T. W. (2000). Social Dynamics of Aggressive and Disruptive Behavior in School: Implications for Behavior Consultation. *Journal of Educational and Psychological Consultation, 11*(3), 299–321.

Felix, E., and M. Furlong. (2008). Best Practices in Bullying Prevention. In A. Thomas and J. Grimes (Eds.), *Best Practices in School Psychology V* (pp. 1,279–89). Bethesda, MD: National Association of School Psychologists.

Fields, L. (2002, July/August). Handling Student Fights: Advice for Teachers and Administrators. *The Clearing House*, pp. 324–26.

Foster, D., and J. Prodis. (1998, May 23). Warning Signs Were Many before Rampage. *Pittsburgh Post-Gazette*, p. 8.

Gilness, J. (2003). How to Integrate Character Education into the Curriculum. *Phi Delta Kappan, 85*, 243–45.

Goldstein, A. P., R. Sprafkin, J. Gershaw, and P. Klein. (1984). *Skillstreaming the Adolescent*. Champaign, IL: Research Press.

Gould, M. S., and R. A. Kramer. (2001). Youth Suicide Prevention. *Suicide and Life-Threatening Behavior, 13*, 6–31.

Greenstone, J. L., and S. C. Leviton. (2002). *Elements of Crisis Intervention*. South Melbourne, Victoria, Australia: Brooks/Cole.

Gregory, A., and M. B. Ripski. (2008). Adolescent Trust in Teachers: Implications for Behavior in the High School Classroom. *School Psychology Review, 37*(3), 337–53.

Gunderson, D. (2005). Who Was Jeff Weise? Retrieved from http://news .minnesota.publicradio.org/features/2005/03/22_ap_redlake.

Gust-Brey, K., and T. Cross. (1999). An Examination of the Literature Base on the Suicidal Behaviors of Gifted Students [Electronic Version]. *Roeper Review, 22*(1), 28–36.

Haggerty, R. J., L. R. Sherrod, N. Garmezy, and M. Rutter (Eds.). (1994). *Stress, Risk, and Resilience in Children and Adolescents.* Cambridge, UK: Cambridge University Press.

Havens, L. L. (1999). Excerpts from an Academic Conference and Recognition of Suicidal Risks through the Psychological Examination. In D. G. Jacobs (Ed.), *Guide to Suicide Assessment and Intervention* (pp. 210–23). San Francisco: Jossey-Bass.

Hays, K. (1998, May 22). Boy Accused of Killing Teacher Held for Trial. *Indiana Gazette*, p. 4.

Hewitt, B., V. Bane, R. Arias, K. Bates, C. Clark, T. Cunneff, L. Stambler, and L. Kramer. (1999, May 3). Sorrow and Outrage. *People, 51*(16), 95–102.

Hewitt, B., J. Harmes, and B. Stewart. (1997, November 3). The Avenger. *People, 48*(18), 116–22.

Holt, M. K., and M. A. Keyes. (2004). Teachers' Attitudes toward Bullying. In D. L. Espelage and S. M. Swearer (Eds.), *Bullying in American Schools* (pp. 121–39). Mahwah, NJ: Lawrence Erlbaum.

Horne, A. M., P. Orpinas, D. Newman-Carlson, and C. L. Bartolomucci. (2004). Elementary School Bully Busters Program: Understanding Why Children Bully and What to Do about It. In D. L. Espelage and S. M. Swearer (Eds.), *Bullying in American Schools* (pp. 297–325). Mahwah, NJ: Lawrence Erlbaum.

Jaksec, C. M., R. F. Dedrick, and R. B. Weinberg. (2000). Classroom Teachers' Ratings of the Acceptability of Crisis Intervention Services. *Traumatology, 6*(9), 9–23.

Joiner, T. E. (2009). Suicide Prevention in Schools as Viewed through the Interpersonal-Psychological Theory of Suicidal Behavior. *School Psychology Review, 38*(2), 244–48.

Jones, S. E., C. J. Fisher, B. Z. Greene, M. F. Hertz, and J. Pritzl. (2007). Healthy and Safe School Environment, Part 1: Results from the School Health Policies and Programs Study 2006. *Journal of School Health, 77*(8), 522–43.

Kalafat, J., and P. J. Lazarus. (2002). Suicide Prevention in Schools. In S. E. Brock, P. J. Lazarus, and S. R. Jimerson (Eds.), *Best Practices in School Crisis Prevention and Intervention* (pp. 211–23). Bethesda, MD: National Association of School Psychologists.

Kam, C., M. T. Greenberg, and C. A. Kusche. (2004). Sustained Effects of the PATHS Curriculum on the Social and Psychological Adjustment of Children in Special Education [Electronic Version]. *Journal of Emotional and Behavioral Disorders*, *12*(2), 66–78.

Kass, S. (2000, June). Homicidal Thoughts Are Not Uncommon among Teens, Study Says. *Monitor on Psychology*, 14.

Kendall, P. C., and L. Braswell. (1993). *Cognitive Behavioral Therapy for Impulsive Children*. New York: Guilford.

Kusche, C. A., and M. T. Greenberg. (1994). *The PATHS Curriculum*. Seattle: Development Research Press.

Lamden, A. M., M. J. King, and R. K. Goldman. (2002). Divorce: Crisis Intervention and Prevention with Children of Divorce and Remarriage. In J. Sandoval (Ed.), *Handbook of Crisis Intervention and Prevention in the Schools* (pp. 83–104). Mahwah, NJ: Lawrence Erlbaum.

Landau, S., R. Milich, M. J. Harris, and S. E. Larson. (2001). "You Really Don't Know How Much It Hurts": Children's and Preservice Teachers' Reactions to Childhood Teasing. *School Psychology Review*, *30*(3), 329–43.

Leary, M. R., R. M. Kowalski, L. Smith, and S. Phillips. (2003). Teasing, Rejection, and Violence: Case Studies of the School Shootings. *Aggressive Behavior*, *29*, 202–14.

Lehman, E. B., and C. J. Erdwins. (2004). The Social and Emotional Adjustment of Young, Intellectually Gifted Children. In S. M. Moon (Ed.), *Social/Emotional Issues, Underachievement, and Counseling of Gifted Students* (pp. 1–8). Thousand Oaks, CA: Corwin.

Levy, M. (2003, April 24). Student Kills Principal, Self inside Pennsylvania Junior High School. *Detnews.com*. Retrieved from www.detnews.com/2003/schools/0304/24/nation-146249.htm.

Limber, S. P. (2004). Implementation of the Olweus Bullying Prevention Program in American Schools: Lessons Learned from the Field. In D. L. Espelage and S. M. Swearer (Eds.), *Bullying in American Schools* (pp. 351–63). Mahwah, NJ: Lawrence Erlbaum.

Malthe, J., R. Riley, C. R. Hall, and J. Adams. (1998, December). 4 Schools, 5 Shooters, 59 Victims. *The Courier Journal*. Retrieved from www.courier-journal.com/cjextra/schoolshoot/SCHthefacts.html#kentucky.

McGinnis, E., and A. P. Goldstein. (1990a). *Skillstreaming the Elementary School Child*. Champaign, IL: Research Press. First edition printed in 1984.

McGinnis, E., and A. P. Goldstein. (1990b). *Skillstreaming in Early Childhood*. Champaign, IL: Research Press. First edition printed in 1984.

McLaughlin, C. S., R. J. Kubick, and M. Lewis. (2002). Best Practices in Promoting Safe Schools. In A. Thomas and J. Grimes (Eds.), *Best Practices in School Psychology IV* (pp. 1,181–94). Bethesda, MD: National Association of School Psychologists.

Military Child Initiative. (2010). School Connectedness: Extending Connections to Military Children. Retrieved from www.jhsph.edu/mci/resources/Exec_Summary_R3.pdf.

Military Child Initiative Home Page. (2010). Retrieved from www.jhsph.edu/mci/.

Mulvey, E. P., and E. Cauffman. (2001). The Inherent Limits of Predicting School Violence. *American Psychologist, 56*(10), 797–802.

Myrick, R. D. (2002). Peer Mediation and Conflict Resolution. In S. Brock, P. Lazarus, and S. Jimerson (Eds.), *Best Practices in School Crisis Prevention and Intervention* (pp. 191–209). Bethesda, MD: National Association of School Psychologists.

National Association of School Psychologists. (2009). *The PREPaRE School Crisis Prevention and Intervention Training Curriculum.* Bethesda, MD: Author.

Nickerson, A. B., and E. D. Slater. (2009). School and Community Violence and Victimization as Predictors of Adolescent Suicidal Behavior. *School Psychology Review, 38*(2), 218–32.

Olweus, D., S. P. Limber, N. Mullin-Rindler, N. Riese, V. Flerx, and M. Snyder. (2003). *Olweus Bullying Prevention Program Training Manual.* Clemson, SC: Authors.

Osher, D., K. Dwyer, and S. Jackson. (2004). *Safe, Supportive, and Successful Schools: Step by Step.* Longmont, CO: Sopris West.

Paine, C. (1998). Tragedy Response and Healing: Springfield Unites. *Communique, 7*(3), 16–17.

Paine, C. K. (2002). Preparing and Managing School Crises. In M. R. Shinn, H. M. Walker, and G. Stoner (Eds.), *Interventions for Academic and Behavior Problems II* (pp. 993–1,017). Bethesda, MD: National Association of School Psychologists.

Paine, S., and C. K. Paine. (2002). Promoting Safety and Success in School by Developing Students' Strengths. In M. R. Shinn, H. M. Walker, and G. Stoner (Eds.), *Interventions for Academic and Behavior Problems II* (pp. 89–108). Bethesda, MD: National Association of School Psychologists.

Palmatier, L. L. (1998). *Crisis Counseling for a Quality School Community.* Washington, DC: Accelerated Development.

Paris, N. J. (1999). *Classroom Crisis Counseling in the Aftermath of School Violence*. Paper presented at the Annual Conference of the Louisiana School Psychologists Association, Lafayette, LA (ERIC Document Reproduction Service No. ED 442043).

Pedersen, D., and S. Van Boven. (1997, December 15). Tragedy in a Small Place. *Newsweek*, 6(14), 30–31.

Pitcher, G. D., and S. Poland. (1992). *Crisis Intervention in the Schools*. New York: Guilford.

Poland, S. (1989). *Suicide Intervention in the Schools*. New York: Guilford.

Poland, S. (1994). The Role of School Crisis Intervention Teams to Prevent and Reduce School Violence and Trauma [Electronic Version]. *School Psychology Review*, 23(2), 175–90.

Poland, S., and R. Lieberman. (2002). Best Practices in Suicide Intervention. In A. Thomas and J. Grimes (Eds.), *Best Practices in School Psychology IV* (pp. 1,151–65). Bethesda, MD: National Association of School Psychologists.

Poland, S., and R. Lieberman. (2004). NEAT Supports Nebraska Schools Following Suicide Cluster. *Communique*, 32(8), 21–22.

Poland, S., G. Pitcher, and P. M. Lazarus. (2002). Best Practices in Crisis Prevention and Management. In A. Thomas and J. Grimes (Eds.), *Best Practices in School Psychology IV* (pp. 1,057–79). Bethesda, MD: National Association of School Psychologists.

Reddy, M., R. Borum, J. Berglund, B. Vossekuil, R. Fein, and W. Modzeleski. (2001). Evaluating Risk for Targeted Violence in Schools: Comparing Risk Assessment, Threat Assessment, and Other Approaches. *Psychology in the Schools*, 38(2), 157–72.

Saillant, C., and A. Covarrubias. (2008). Oxnard School Shooting Called a Hate Crime. Retrieved from www.latimes.com/news/local/la-me-oxnard 15feb15,0,7958737,full.story.

Screening for Mental Health. (2010). *SOS Signs of Suicide Prevention Program*. Wellesley, MA: Author.

Seifer, R., K. Gouley, A. Miller, and A. Zakriski. (2004). Implementation of the PATHS Curriculum in an Urban Elementary School [Electronic Version]. *Early Education and Development*, 15(4), 471–85.

Shure, M. (2001). *I Can Problem Solve (ICPS): An Interpersonal Cognitive Problem-Solving Program*. Champaign, IL: Research Press.

Staudacher, C. (1994). *A Time to Grieve*. San Francisco: Harper.

Steele, W., and M. Raider. (1991). *Working with Families in Crisis: School-Based Intervention*. New York: Guilford.

Suldo, S. M., A. A. Friedrich, T. White, J. Farmer, D. Minch, and J. Michalowski. (2009). Teacher Support and Adolescents' Subjective Well-Being: A Mixed-Methods Investigation. *School Psychology Review*, *38*(1), 67–85.

Swearer, S. M., L. Espelage, and S. A. Napolitano. (2009). *Bullying Prevention and Intervention: Realistic Strategies for Schools*. New York: Guilford.

Swearer, S. M., R. K. Turner, J. Givens, and W. S. Pollack. (2008). "You're So Gay!": Do Different Forms of Bullying Matter for Adolescent Males? *School Psychology Review*, *37*(2), 160–73.

Taub, J. (2001). Evaluation of the Second Step Violence Prevention Program at a Rural Elementary School. *School Psychology Review*, *31*(2), 186–200.

Thombs, D. L. (2000). A Retrospective Study of DARE: Substantive Effects Not Detected in Undergraduates. *Journal of Alcohol and Drug Education*, *46*, 27–40.

Tizon, A. (1997, February 23). What Has This Town Become? *Seattle Times*, pp. A12, A18.

Trump, K. S. (2002, May). Proactive School Security and Crisis Preparedness Strategies in the Wake of Terrorism. Presentation to the ARIN Intermediate Unit, Indiana, PA.

U.S. Department of Education. (2006a). Creating Emergency Management Plans. *Emergency Response and Crisis Management Technical Assistance Center ERCM Express*, *2*(8). Washington, DC: Author.

U.S. Department of Education. (2006b). The National Incident Management System. *Emergency Response and Crisis Management Technical Assistance Center ERCM Express*, *2*(6). Washington, DC: Author.

Van Schoiack-Edstrom, L., K. S. Frey, and K. Beland. (2002). Changing Adolescents' Attitudes about Relational and Physical Aggression: An Evaluation of a School-Based Intervention. *School Psychology Review*, *31*(2), 201–16.

Vossekuil, B., R. Fein, M. Reddy, R. Borum, and W. Modzeleski. (2004). *The Final Report and Findings of the Safe School Initiative: Implications for the Prevention of School Attacks in the United States*. Washington, DC: U.S. Department of Education, Office of Elementary and Secondary Education, Safe and Drug-Free Schools Program, and U.S. Secret Service National Threat Assessment Center.

Weisz, J. R., B. Weiss, S. S. Han, D. A. Granger, and T. Morton. (1995). Effects of Psychotherapy with Children and Adolescents Revisited: A Meta-Analysis of Treatment Outcome Studies [Electronic Version]. *Psychological Bulletin*, *117*(3), 450–68.

West, S. L., and K. K. O'Neal. (2004). Project DARE Outcome Effectiveness Revisited. *American Journal of Public Health*, *94*(6), 1,027–29.

Yule, W. (2001). When Disaster Strikes: The Need to Be Wise before the Event: Crisis Intervention with Children [Electronic Version]. *Advances in Mind-Body Medicine*, *17*(3), 191–97.

Zagelbaum, A., C. Alexander, and T. Kruczek. (2002). *The 9/11 Tragedy: Some School-Based Initiatives*. Paper presented at the Annual Conference of the American Psychological Association, Chicago, IL (ERIC Document Reproduction Service No. ED473630).

Good Behavior Game, 130–131
grief. *See* death
guns. *See* crisis events, role of
    firearms in

hostile/aggressive students, 71–92;
    confrontation of, 73; coping with,
    74–77, 81–82; physical contact
    with, 75, 82; signs of danger in,
    72; thought processes of, 90–91

I Can Problem Solve, 130

laws and regulations, 69, 83–84,
    120–122, 127, 145

materials and packaged programs,
    181–182
medication, 98
memorials, 52–53
National Association of School
    Psychologists, 69, 117, 123, 124
National Crisis Prevention Institute,
    75. 82, 123–124
National Incident Management
    System (NIMS), 145
natural disasters, 37–39
non–English speaking students,
    support during a crisis, 160

Olweus Bullying Prevention
    Program, 84, 143
organizations and websites, 173–
    181
ostracism. *See* bullying

paraprofessionals, role in crisis
    prevention, 17
parent-teacher conferences, 137–141
parents. *See* families

PATHS, 130–131
peer mediation. *See* conflict
    resolution
peer relations, role in crisis events,
    9, 82, 97, 105
physical disabilities. *See* disabilities
Positive Behavioral Support, 143–
    144
poverty, role in crisis events, 9
PREPaRE, vii, 124
problem solving, as crisis
    prevention, 84, 85, 109, 115,
    129–132, 155
privacy. *See* confidentiality
professional development, 82,
    122–125

referral to mental health practitioner;
    after crisis event, 155; how to
    make a, 162–164; problems in
    making, 164–165; for student at
    risk, 112–113, 161; for student's
    reaction to death, 53–55; for
    suspicion of suicide, 62–65
relational aggression. *See* bullying
religion, role in crisis prevention, 11
resilience, 57, 61
respect, role in crisis prevention, 78,
    105, 116–118
rumor control. *See* communication

Safe School Initiative, 9, 10, 13,
Second Step, 130–131
societal issues, as factors in crisis,
    13–14
SOS Program. *See* suicide, school-
    wide prevention programs
sports, role in crisis prevention, 11
stress, management of, 23, 61, 106,
    107, 131, 135, 157; signs of, 3,

About the Author

Victoria B. Damiani is professor emeritus of educational and school psychology at Indiana University of Pennsylvania. She holds a doctoral degree in school psychology from the College of William and Mary and is a nationally certified school psychologist. Dr. Damiani has been director of both the IUP Child Study Center and IUP Center for Gifted Education and is a past president of the Association of School Psychologists of Pennsylvania. Her research interests include school mental health and crisis intervention, families of exceptional children, and gifted education.